The Promise of Deliverance

The Promise of Deliverance

Reading Second Isaiah

Michael Casey, OCSO

ORBIS BOOKS
www.orbisbooks.com

ORBIS BOOKS
www.orbisbooks.com

Fathers and Brothers
MARYKNOLL

Founded in 1970, Orbis Books endeavors to publish works that enlighten the mind, nourish the spirit, and challenge the conscience. The publishing arm of the Maryknoll Fathers and Brothers, Orbis seeks to explore the global dimensions of the Christian faith and mission, to invite dialogue with diverse cultures and religious traditions, and to serve the cause of reconciliation and peace. The books published reflect the views of their authors and do not represent the official position of the Maryknoll Society. To learn more about Maryknoll and Orbis Books, please visit our website at www.maryknollsociety.org.

Published by Orbis Books, Box 302, Maryknoll, NY 10545-0302.

Imprimi potest, Abbot Steele Hartmann, 4 June 2020

Manufactured in the United States of America

Library of Congress Cataloging-in-Publication Data

Names: Casey, Michael, 1942– author.
Title: The promise of deliverance : reading Second Isaiah / Michael Casey, OCSO.
Description: Maryknoll : Orbis Books, [2021] | Includes bibliographical references and index. | Summary: “The Promise of Deliverance is a series of reflections on important themes of Isaiah 40-55, intended to add value to the reader’s approach to the biblical text”— Provided by publisher.
Identifiers: LCCN 2020036328 (print) | LCCN 2020036329 (ebook) | ISBN 9781626984080 (trade paperback) | ISBN 9781608338726 (epub)
Subjects: LCSH: Bible. Isaiah, XL-LV—Theology—Meditations.
Classification: LCC BS1520 .C37 2021 (print) | LCC BS1520 (ebook) | DDC
224/.106—dc23
LC record available at https://lccn.loc.gov/2020036328
LC ebook record available at https://lccn.loc.gov/2020036329

Written during the reign of Coronavirus

Dedicated to its victims

Contents

Introduction

Since the work of Bernhard Duhm toward the end of the nineteenth century, it is widely but not universally accepted that the Book of Isaiah is composed of three distinct segments: Chapters 1—39, 40—55, and 56—66. There is a possibility that the distinction is not as clear-cut as many would like, granted the long lines of transmission through which the text has passed.[1] While experts will continue to debate the issues, often on the basis of ideological preferences, there is value in approaching Second Isaiah, as a separate entity, composed between the fall of Jerusalem in 587 BCE and the Decree of Cyrus some fifty years later in 539 BCE. This is not necessarily to deny that Second Isaiah is the work of many hands or that it incorporates literary units that originally may have been independent. Nor is it to disregard the many linkages with First Isaiah (composed in the eighth and seventh centuries) and Third Isaiah (compiled after the return from the exile).

---

[1] Remembering that the division of the biblical books into discrete chapters occurred only in the Middle Ages. Chapter division is usually attributed to Stephen Langton (1150–1228), Archbishop of Canterbury. Verse-division appeared first in the printed edition of the Bible by Robert Estienne in 1555.

These sixteen chapters are among the Old Testament passages most frequently cited in the books of the New Testament.[2] The Gospels begin by presenting John the Baptist in terms drawn from the opening lines of Second Isaiah and reach their culmination in narrating the passion of Jesus and trying to explain it in terms of the Suffering Servant of Isa 52—53. Along with Deuteronomy and the Book of Psalms, Second Isaiah is a major source of the theology of the New Testament, not only in content, but also in terms of its rhetorical power and affective warmth. The New Testament is proclamation: its message is kerygma. It is not mere narrative or lawmaking. It has a strong prophetic voice, and that voice announces not doom and gloom but "good news," as does this prophet. In both the New Testament and Second Isaiah, there is challenge and also rebuke, but the prevailing message is positive. Both speak of a loving and compassionate God who seeks to undo the harms that humanity has inflicted upon itself by being seduced away from the path of worship in spirit and in truth.

The people deported to Babylon were a much-reduced population. According to Jeremiah, those deported between 587 and 571 BCE numbered no more than forty-six hundred (cf. Jer 52:28–30). If this number refers only to adult males, then together with women and children, the exiles may have been as many as twenty thousand—no more than a small crowd watching a football game. They were conscious not only of their fewness, but also of their impotence. It is likely that their thoughts were dominated by an overwhelming grief for all they had lost: family, friends, possessions, national identity and pride, religious tradition and worship. No doubt they experienced the interior emptiness that follows the total deconstruction of a familiar world. For many, it must have seemed that Judah would go the way of the

---

[2] There are 29 quotations of Second Isaiah and 143 "allusions and verbal parallels" identified in the third edition of *The Greek New Testament* published by the United Bible Societies in 1983.

Northern Kingdom that had been lost to Assyria, and that there would be no future to their race or their religion. Children would be born and raised among the remnant of a people whose only hope was assimilation. Contact with their long tradition would be lost; all they could aspire to was to be accepted as "normal" Babylonians. It would be only a matter of time before they bowed down to Marduk.

The Babylonian Exile lasted some fifty years. If we superimpose a similar period on the life of the contemporary church, we may well find that although we have not been deported to Babylon, many of us have experienced an acute sense of displacement from where we were half a century ago.[3] Most of our certainties have been exploded, and in many cases the thread of continuity has been broken. Scientific advances and historical criticism have exposed the temerity of many of the facile assumptions we employed to reinforce our faith. Secularization has brought into question the relevance of religious institutions. Aggressive atheism tries to convince us that belief in God is unintelligent. Religious fanaticism has undermined our notion that dedicated religious people are always good people. Sexual abuse, financial finagling, and administrative toleration of crimes have scuttled any claim that the Church is to be known by its holiness. Welcome to Babylon.

---

[3] "The metaphor of exile may be useful to American Christians as a way of understanding the social context of the church in American culture [and beyond]. The exile of the contemporary American church is that we are bombarded by definitions of reality that are fundamentally alien to the gospel, definitions of reality that come from the military-industrial-scientific empire, which may be characterized as 'consumer capitalism.' In a variety of ways the voice of this empire wants to reshape our values, fears and dreams in ways that are fundamentally opposed to the voice of the gospel." Walter Brueggemann, *Hopeful Imagination: Prophetic Voices in Exile* (Philadelphia: Fortress Press, 1986), 92. See also, by the same author, *Virus as a Summons to Faith: Biblical Reflections in a Time of Loss, Grief, and Uncertainty* (New York: Cascade Books, 2020).

The Catholic remnant remains as much in need of the prophetic word of hope as the remnant of Judah. Even those of us blessed with the gift of a holy obstinacy may sometimes feel a sense of loss. This is not to say that the changes wrought in the wake of the Second Vatican Council were not helpful. They were more than that; they were necessary and providential. Undeniably, there was collateral damage. Much of this can be traced to an insufficient preparation, not only of the people in the pews, but also of those who were supposed to support them and guide them through the time of transition. This is not to point the finger of blame; the task was formidable, given the massive changes in most cultures these past fifty years.[4] Many burned themselves out attempting to bridge the gap between the immovable past and the ever-moving present; others fell into disrepute by seeming to change too quickly, or too slowly. There are polarizing tensions in God's people today that were unknown half a century ago.

We all appreciate that it is hard for a long-lasting institution to change quickly, since it can move only at the speed of its slowest members. Saint Paul experienced this in his dealings with the elders of the Jerusalem church. This means that a gap tends to open between what the group has to offer and what

---

[4] Even before the coronavirus pitched its tent in our midst and the effects of climate change began to appear, it is obvious that secular society itself has changed much in the last fifty years both at the political and geopolitical levels. There has been an explosion of information technology and a resulting revolution in the way we do and view things. In a moment of desperation, I recently read a spy novel written in 1980. It was describing a vastly different world. The Cold War was still raging. There were no computers or cell phones or Internet. You found your way without the benefit of GPS, and at the airport there was little by way of security. The issues that dominate our conversations today went unmentioned. Those of us who lived through this period simply went with the flow and scarcely noticed the radicalism of what was changing around us. We may have come to the conclusion that others were changing but were less aware of inevitably shifting attitudes in ourselves. Only in retrospect are we stunned by the depth and extent of change.

the membership requires to sustain its life. The inevitable result is that even the most loyal among ordinary members will often go shopping to find some supplement to what they are being offered officially. Sometimes they end up in a cul-de-sac in which progress peters out. But others, inspired by good zeal, lay their hands on hidden treasures and bring them into the light. In today's Church—much more than fifty years ago—people are discovering for themselves the value of such interior practices as meditation and *lectio divina*, in helping them to move into an authentic practice of prayer. This, in turn, motivates and empowers them to find new ways of living their faith and encourages them to assume new roles in giving external expression to what they hold dear.

Finding in the Scriptures a pathway to a more abundant life not only makes one's personal life more meaningful but inevitably leads us back to the mystical Communion of Saints and, perhaps, to a fuller appreciation of the institutional Church. In particular, *lectio divina* may help us to leap over the overzealous moralism that has dominated Catholic thinking for the last few centuries. It places an emphasis on the Church as a school of mysticism, with an emphasis on the experience of coming closer to God. It is not only a matter of upgrading our public morals. It is not merely a question of intellectual learning so that we have all the right answers. It is more a question of a burgeoning affectivity in defiance of prevailing feelinglessness. Perhaps we grew up with the slogan "Faith not feeling," but faith without feeling is a void. Feeling indicates that we are alive, whether what we are experiencing is pleasant or challenging. Even when everything seems to be going well, our faith may lead us into an experience of desolation. This feeling, although disturbing, is better than no-feeling. Almost always it is a providential carrier of the truth. If we respond to it, it will almost certainly lead us to a better place. Our faith can never be merely an intellectual exercise. Even an apparently negative feeling may well be, not the end of prayer, but its beginning—not a sign of decline but a pointer to a more solid way ahead. The fire alarm that wakes us up is a friend, not an enemy.

In trying to find our feet spiritually, we will find Second Isaiah a good companion and mentor. His message is addressed to those who feel somewhat alienated from God because the social order that sustained the relationship has broken down. His response is to point both to the power of God to accomplish good for us, and to the divine compassion which exceeds every human experience of tenderness. And he does this in a way that touches the heart. In fact, this is his mandate: To speak to the heart of Jerusalem (cf. Isa 40:2). To spend a few months in the company of this most perceptive of prophets probably won't teach us any new dogmas, but it may well kindle in us a greater sense of the subtle involvement of God in our life, working to bring us to a point of vision that is beyond anything we could imagine for ourselves.

* * *

For the purposes of this book, I am taking a simple approach, regarding the chapters as a unity—even though there is a change in tone after Chapter 48, and the four passages designated as "Servant Songs" may be interpolations. For the sake of convenience, I refer to the prophet Second Isaiah as its "author"—although I understand that this role may well include the functions of writing, compiling, and editing, perhaps on different occasions and by several persons. I am conscious that such an uncomplicated view leaves many questions not only unanswered but also unasked. Such is life. I do not see the text of Second Isaiah as a Teutonic treatise following strict sequential logic, but as a message of hope and comfort, put together from a variety of sources following a circular, right-brain progression. My principal purpose in writing is to assist the reader to engage with the book through a process of *lectio divina*, without being drawn to wandering down the seductive byways of scholarly debate—to be more aware of the tides than the eddies, as it were.

Without underestimating the importance of historical-critical study, this present work aims at facilitating a kind of conversation between the text and its contemporary readers—particularly those who are reading it not for the purpose of academic scrutiny, but to hear in the text a comforting and challenging word that speaks to each in their own particular situation. This is not a fundamentalist approach. It involves trying to come to as accurate an understanding of the text as is possible, given each person's concrete circumstances. What is distinctive about *lectio divina* is that, while paying attention to the text, the reader also allows the mind to roam through other books of the Bible and other sources of wisdom, including personal experience. It invites more participants to the party in the hope that approaching the text from a variety of standpoints will allow the reader to become aware of subtler nuances that otherwise might be missed. It is a fuller, ampler reading. It is not trying to prove anything; it is intended only for personal growth in wisdom.

An example of how personal experience allows us to become sensitive to less obvious aspects of the text can be seen in the way our years of reading the Bible can enrich our present understanding. Readers who are familiar with the Book of Psalms will quickly arrive at the conclusion that there are many parallels between Second Isaiah and the Psalter, as demonstrated by the marginal references in many editions of the Bible. There are more than a hundred linkages between the two books, because although individual psalms were composed over several centuries, they were compiled into the existing collection at some time in the postexilic period. Many psalms were in circulation at the time of the exile. Second Isaiah was thus probably at least passively familiar with some of them and, perhaps unconsciously, drew from them both in content and style. It is not impossible that influence went in both directions. While writing this book, I kept hearing echoes of the prophet in the usual psalms of the liturgy; the two parts of Scripture sparked off each other in a process of mutual enrichment.

Although Second Isaiah was originally composed in and for a particular historical setting, its inclusion in the biblical canon attached to First Isaiah seems to indicate that its message has a broader application than simply the return of the exiles from Babylon. Its message was reinterpreted to evoke the eschatological intervention of God in the ultimate act of deliverance; as such, it applies as much to us as it did to Second Isaiah's contemporaries. We know, as Haggai indicates, that the return of some of the exiles to the land was not a glorious triumph. It was a meager beginning to the ongoing action of God—a symbol and pledge of what was to come in the final age. "The discrepancy between what happened after the exile and the prophet's eschatological description of God's will is not a criticism of the truth of the promise, but rather an indication of how little the exilic community partook of the promised reality."[5] This message is addressed not only to the scattered remnant of Judah and its returnees, but also to us, who live in such different times and in such particular circumstances. It relays to us God's unswerving commitment not only to overcoming the obstacles that beset us but also to bringing us all together to eternal life. In particular, Second Isaiah contains an emergent notion of universalism, whereby salvation is not limited to Israel but offered to all. It references "a confessional community rather than a nation state, and therefore community adherence to which can come about by personal decision rather than by ascription."[6] The good news of

---

[5] Brevard S. Childs, *Introduction to the Old Testament* (London: SCM Press, 1979), 327.

[6] Joseph Blenkinsopp, *Isaiah 40—55: A New Translation with Introduction and Commentary* (New York: Doubleday, 2000), 116. The expansion of the divine self-revelation made to Israel so that it is given to all nations represents a substantial step forward away from tribalism toward the notion of a more inclusive religion. This movement illustrates the suggestion that greater inclusivism is a key indicator of moral progress. See Allen Buchanan and Russell Powell, *The Evolution of Moral Progress: A Biocultural Theory* (New York: Oxford University Press, 2018).

Second Isaiah is meant for all nations, and its message of comfort is for all peoples. As Abraham Heschel notes,

> The message of Second Isaiah, as he is conventionally called, is of no age. It is prophecy tempered with human tears, mixed with a joy that heals all scars, clearing a way for understanding the future in spite of the present. No words have ever gone further in offering comfort when the sick world cries.[7]

We must never forget that Second Isaiah was written over two and a half millennia ago. It breathes an atmosphere that is strange to us, and we can hear its message only by transposing it into a different key. The effort is well worthwhile. It is astonishing that, so long ago, such a sophisticated theology could be formulated and expressed so elegantly. This is one of the most compelling parts of the Old Testament. It has been described as "the zenith of Yahweh's revelation in the OT."[8] The prophet sees his proclamation as "good news"—we, likewise, may well regard his work as a precursor to the gospel. Spending a few months wandering around the text, imbibing its spirit and pondering its message, will be for most of us a rich experience that will generously repay whatever we have invested in it.

Second Isaiah has a very coherent theology, as represented schematically in Figure 1. It is a firm statement of monotheism. There is only one God, the God of Israel. This transcendent God must be seen as the creator of heaven and earth—a proposition familiar to us from the opening chapters of the Book of Genesis, which attained its final form only about the time that Second Isaiah appeared. God has absolute and complete dominion and is, therefore, the Lord of history who has the power to influence

---

[7] Abraham Joshua Heschel, *The Prophets* (Peabody, MA: Hendrickson, 2009), 145.

[8] R. Reed Lessing, *Isaiah 40—55* (St. Louis: Concordia, 2011), 3.

events and, thus, is able to predict what will happen. Whatever God promises can be accomplished. Therefore, Israel will be preserved and will return from exile. Babylon will be destroyed, and to effect this, the campaign of Cyrus of Persia will be successful. As the only God, the God of Israel must also be the God of all nations, to whom all must turn to find salvation, which means that they will attach themselves to Israel, God's servant. Thus, Israel's mission is to be "a light for the Gentiles," and to do this, Israel must be preserved and return from exile. Thus God accomplishes the plan initiated in creation. Meanwhile, idols are nothing. Those who worship them are stupid, and both idols and their devotees are doomed to ultimate destruction.

This book is envisaged as a companion to the biblical text, not its replacement. It is not a commentary on Second Isaiah. It is a book of reflection that weaves in and out and round about the biblical text. It is intended to support your own reflections and responses and to begin a conversation that embraces also the reality of your own life. It aspires to help you, the reader, to appreciate the timely message that the prophet offers. The method to be employed is simply to take a number of themes that are important for understanding the text and reflect on them in a circular fashion, pulling together elements from different parts of the book and adding a few other considerations to the mix. It is hoped that in this process we will become more sensitive to the themes as we encounter them in our reading of Second Isaiah and move on to a richer understanding of the prophet's message. In my mind, the whole process could be spread over several months and, ideally, would involve several rereadings of the biblical text until it becomes familiar.

Instead of retranslating the text of Second Isaiah, I have decided to use the translation included in the Geneva Bible of 1562,[9] for three related reasons. First, I hope that the archaic

---

[9] *The Bible and Holy Scriptures conteyned in the Olde and New Testament translated according to the Ebrve and Greke and conferred with the*

THE GOD OF ISRAEL
is
CREATOR
with
TOTAL DOMINION
LORD OF HISTORY
THE ONLY GOD
has POWER to SAVE
FAITHFUL to PROMISES
has POWER to PREDICT
GOD OF ALL NATIONS
ALL must come for SALVATION
Attach themselves to ISRAEL
Israel has a MISSION
Israel will be PRESERVED
Israel will return from EXILE
BABYLON will fall
CYRUS will succeed
IDOLS ARE FUTILE
Idolatry is senseless

style of this translation will alert the reader to the fact that the biblical book was written two and a half thousand years ago in a culture and political situation far different from anything that we have experienced, and in a language with which most of us are unfamiliar. I try to keep reminding the reader that we have to work hard to arrive at an honest interpretation of the text. It is foreign to us, and we have to read it carefully.

The second reason for using this translation is to make clear the distinction between the biblical text and my commentary. What I have to say does not demand the same respect as what Second Isaiah says. I should add that very occasionally I have made some slight changes to remove obscurity, but mostly I have allowed to stand what may seem to us an eccentric style. I presume the long-dead editors have no objection to this.

A third reason for using an unfamiliar text is that this ancient translation provides a basis for comparison with newer renderings. Comparing two translations can be a partial remedy for those unable to approach the text in the original. Going from one version to the other is a basic way of meditating on the text. Reading the same text in one version and then in another tends to set dormant thoughts astir and open up some space in our otherwise torpid minds into which inspiration can slip. This method initiates us into the process of close reading; as we make comparisons, we begin to pay attention to the minor differences between the versions, leading us into a state of wonderment. We try on the different readings, as we would a new pair of shoes, to see which one speaks to us more clearly and more dearly. Which one throws a fairer light on our personal experience? We might enhance the effect by reading the texts aloud, listening to their poetry, succumbing to the charm of the biblical eloquence.

Because Hebrew is a Semitic language, there are many

---

best translations in divers languages, with most profitable annotations upon all the hard places and other things of great importance as may appear in the epistle to the reader, printed at Geneva, MDLXII.

differences in vocabulary and grammar from what is usual in the Indo-European languages that are more familiar to us. In particular, the standard translation of certain Hebrew words usually does not coincide with the range of meanings and associations with the original. I have decided to presume on the readers' indulgence by explaining some key words in greater detail. Usually I cite a single form (or lexeme) within a word family to refer to the whole group of associated terms. In my transcription of Hebrew script, I have adopted simple equivalents, rather than use the more complex systems scholars employ.

A question that often raised its head while I was writing these chapters concerned the inclusion of references to the New Testament. It is true that the primary meaning of the New Testament text needs to be sought in the context of the Hebrew Scriptures of which it is a part. Yet, as a Christian reader, it is impossible for me to read Second Isaiah without calling to mind the New Testament use of this book, or the parallels that exist in the good news that each proclaims. I decided to act as naturally as I could; if a New Testament reference came to my mind, I considered including it. I did not go hunting for examples. Some references to monastic tradition also inevitably find their way into my text.

No doubt for many readers, as for myself, reading Second Isaiah will stir up memories of Handel's "Messiah." It is as though the text suddenly bursts into song before us. I think that the great value in this connection is that it serves as a reminder of the deep affective and emotional tone of many passages in the book. It speaks not only to the mind but also to the heart of Jerusalem. My hope is that these chapters do the same, though perhaps in a minor key.

1

Consolation

The first word of Second Isaiah is "Console." The work is often named simply "The Book of Consolation." The prophet begins his proclamation by placing in the mouth of God the words that provide the mandate for his mission. To the exiles in Babylon, he is to give a message of hope. It will soon become clear that this hope is not based on any residual strength that the people may possess, but entirely on the undeviating and unconditional love borne for them by their God. They are to lift their gaze from the aggrieved contemplation of their own misfortune and ruin, and bring back to their minds the thought of God's capacity to write straight on crooked lines.

> Comfort ye, comfort ye my people, will your God say. Speak comfortably to Jerusalem, and cry unto her, that her warfare is accomplished, that her iniquity is pardoned; for she hath received of the Lord's hand double for all her sins. (Isa 40:1–2)

To get the most out of Second Isaiah, we have to develop the skill of reading it with one eye on the text and the other on our own experience of life, allowing the two to interact and to throw light on each other. It is true that we were not exiled to Babylon. It is also true that sometimes we feel oppressed and constricted by the situation in which we find ourselves, whether this be of our own making or the result of the actions of others. Sometimes we feel alienated from what we intuitively glimpse as a more authentic existence. We may not be forced to make our domicile in Babylon, but that does not prevent us "poor, banished children of Eve" from looking beyond this "valley of tears" to a sphere in which a more abundant life will be ours.

No doubt the theology that the prophet eventually enunciates was known to the exiles on a rational level. What was needed was a stronger infusion of affective warmth into what was left of their religion. Faith has a bad reputation. For many it seems a bare reality—important, but without much in the way of comfort. It can be said, especially when people are enduring hard times, that faith seems like a mere skeleton: necessary but hard, brittle, and mostly invisible. Such reductionism comes from emphasizing the intellectual component of faith and forgetting about its interpersonal dynamism.

Faith is the kindling by which the fire of love is sustained; the two are inseparable. The theological virtue of charity cannot exist without the foundation of faith. But faith is meaningless unless it does what it is meant to do—to set alight the flame of charity and then to keep it burning. Faith without love is dead. We know that we have faith when we experience love. Faith is not the naked reality some presume it to be. The saints and the martyrs who passed through periods of extreme suffering and apparent desolation lived by faith. The desolation was only on the surface. Deep down they were sustained by the infinitely subtle assurance that comes from contact with a loving God. Why otherwise would they sing, "In all these things we have overcome because of him who has loved us"?

I say this to emphasize the importance of consolation in our efforts to live a spiritual life. We cannot long survive in a state of self-imposed exile from God. Like camels, we can cross the desert without drinking for a time, even for an extended time. But not forever. Without a sense of being connected to God, our spiritual life will wither, and our desire to come closer to God will seem no more than a delusion.

The English word "consolation" has at its heart a Sanskrit root: *selh*. This means happiness or good cheer; it is also the foundation of the German word *selig*. To this has been added the Latin prefix, *con-*, signifying that the source of this happiness is the company of someone else. Geoffrey Chaucer gives the meaning of the word as "to have another fellow in his pain" (*Troylus* I.102). In difficult times we find comfort, joy, and even pleasure because we have someone with us who is able to counterbalance our troubles with their solidarity and support.

The message to the exiles is clear. "The Lord will surely comfort Zion, and will look with compassion on all her ruins. He will make her wastelands like the garden of the Lord. Joy and gladness will be found in her, thanksgiving and the sound of singing" (51:3). There is no denial of the disasters that have befallen the people. The reality and the extent of these are recognized. Despite the wreckage of a previous existence and the dissolution of all previous hopes and aspirations, there will be a glorious future—because God has promised it. As for Zion, so for us.

The prophet's mission of consolation is not so much informative as affective. He is to "speak to the heart of Jerusalem" (40:2). To give new heart to the disheartened. As the book proceeds it will become clear that the consoler is very clear-eyed. He is more than the distributor of tear-drying tissues. He seeks gently to help the despondent understand their complicity in their misfortune and at the same time to emphasize that God's role is to lead them forth from the disaster their sins have created.

The prophet's words are designed to mediate an encounter with God. There is no other source of effective consolation. This is because God alone has the power to avenge wrongs done and to bring the exiles back to safety. Every meeting with the one true God brings us the consolation that rekindles our fervor and enables us to reframe the situation in which we find ourselves. If we find ourselves in a state of utter desolation, it is because we have drifted away from God.

So—what of our own situation? There is always comfort available for us, but we have to learn to perceive what is not always apparent at first glance. The traditional Australian aborigines are said to have been able to cross the vast deserts in the continent's center without carrying a lot of luggage. They were able to find water where we would pass by; they made their meals of what we would consider to be inedible. They perceived more than we do and so the desert was a friendly place for them. When we find ourselves passing through long periods in which our inner landscape is barren and seemingly incapable of supporting life, we need to ask ourselves whether this is really so. Perhaps the problem is that we need to begin to see things differently. To evaluate possibilities differently. To accept that change is necessary, change within ourselves. Not in the outside world. In us.

God is present even in the desert. Many times in his writings, Saint Augustine deplores the reality that while God is present to us, we are not present to God. By this he means that we are unable to perceive the presence of God because of hardship, because of distraction, because of a lack of instruction, whereby we do not even know what we are supposed to be looking for. The world is full of interesting things that can easily absorb all our attention. We become preoccupied with what is immediate and visible, and lose contact with the subtle and invisible world of spiritual reality. "For they live among [God's] works, and trust their sense of sight, because what is seen is fair" (Wis 13:7). We do not know where to look. This dilemma was nobly stated by Saint Augustine:

> Late have I loved Thee, O Beauty so ancient and so new; late have I loved Thee! For behold Thou wert within me, and I outside; and I sought Thee outside and in my unloveliness fell upon these lovely things that Thou hast made. Thou wert with me and I was not with Thee. I was

kept from Thee by those things, yet had they not been in Thee, they would not have been at all.[1]

I will go further. It is in the desert, when God seems most absent, that God is especially present. It is often when our carefully planned lives go awry that God makes an appearance. When the defensive bastions of routine and complacency crumble, we begin to see what was hidden for as long as they remained intact. Compensations, substitutes, and distractions populate our inner lives and make them seem, if not interesting, at least not empty. When these disappear—either through involuntary change in our circumstances or because of their innate inability to satisfy our restless hearts—the possibility of a radical change dawns. The impact of this existential emptiness is to make us set out on a search for meaning. We are driven forward by being touched by emptiness. We feel impelled to cast away whatever in our lives is inauthentic and alienating, and then to reach beyond the mundane to discover the foundational truth of our being, the mystery that lies at the heart of every person. That is why, paradoxically, we can say we experience God by experiencing emptiness; God is present to us through absence.

There were external hardships in which the exiles found themselves: the loss of homeland and kindred, the condition of captivity, the prospect of the loss of national identity. Accompanying these difficulties was also an interior loss: the loss of meaning that had come about because of forgetfulness of their own religious heritage and their effective abandonment of God. It was to those suffering from this interior desert that Second Isaiah addressed his message of hope.

Saint Augustine frequently asked himself how God could be present in our world when neither sense nor intellect is able

---

[1] *Confessiones* X.xxvii.38; *Corpus Christianorum: Series Latina* 27, p. 175. Translated by F. J. Sheed, *The Confessions of Saint Augustine* (London: Sheed & Ward, 1944), 188.

to perceive this presence. His answer was both profound and paradoxical. God is present in our world by a perceived absence; God is that which does not register on sense or intellect. God is not an object in our world, alongside other objects. Even if we are wise enough to be able to affirm the existence of an ultimate Absolute, we cannot unaided know its nature. We cannot comprehend what God is like on our own. God is not a thing to be placed under the microscope of our mind and examined. God is objectively absent. Contact is made intersubjectively. God is the "Thou" that mysteriously calls to our "I." We hear this call when we allow ourselves to be moved by God's absence and to begin to desire that absence be transformed into presence. Our grasp of the incompleteness that is the known universe is the stimulus that prompts our search for what is beyond this world. Israel's fault was that it had ceased to listen for God's call, so that when it came it went unanswered. "When I demanded of them, they answered not a word" (Isa 41:28). "Wherefore came I, and there was no man? I called, and none answered" (50:2).

Consider this example. When a person dies, the empty chair in which that person habitually sat shouts more loudly of their presence than when they were actually sitting in it. Or another: the errant son willfully absent from a Mother's Day dinner is probably more present to her mind and heart than his noisy siblings around the table. The elephant in the room that goes unseen. Father Brown, G. K. Chesterton's fictional detective, frequently solved murder mysteries by noticing what didn't happen or what was absent. The dog that didn't bark. God is that which we cannot find in the richly endowed world of space and time, no matter how hard or how intelligently we look. "Truly you are a God who hides, God of Israel and Savior" (Isa 45:15).

The one sure thing that we know is that our means of knowing anything about God are extremely subtle. The apophatic approach of Eastern theologians affirms that it is easier to know what God is not than to know what God is. In this stance, God remains a mystery—something that can be wonderingly contemplated forever with deep satisfaction, but without ever coming to a conclusion or an end. Not a puzzle to be solved but a darkness that is more full of light than the daylight around us. The Western approach of trying to say as much as possible and to define everything within strict rational categories can often seem soulless. Academic theology may entertain the mind but often leaves devotion to starve. True knowledge of God is not intellectual knowledge but the awareness that results from interpersonal experience—made possible by grace.

The experience of God's absence is what arouses in us the desire for God's presence. Paradoxically, hard times may be good for us since they forcefully remind us that we have here no abiding city, but seek one that is to come. Often, when circumstances seem to run against us, we learn skills that enable us to profit when our situation improves. When the sun shines and everything goes well with us, we experience no real need for God, though we may occasionally acknowledge God as a contributor to our success. We don't seek God because we have everything we need. Only when trouble strikes do we come to the realization of the emptiness of self-satisfied existence.

Perhaps this was the way with the people of biblical Israel. They could begin to appreciate God only when contact was broken: when the Temple was defiled and its guaranteed mode of worship destroyed, when they were removed from the land promised to Abraham and his descendants forever, when they were reduced to a servitude like that of their forebears in Egypt. From all that they had lost, Second Isaiah tries to lead them to an appreciation of what still remains—the undeviating love of the God who called and continues to call them. The fire of tribulation can serve to burn away the dross that inevitably accumulates around institutionalized religion. The baubles of tribal belief and ritual must be left aside in favor of a starker and darker but more enduring faith. By hard experience we learn to cling to those elements of our relationship with God that are not subject to the ebb and flow of external circumstance. When all else fails, God remains.

So the work of the prophet is to fan into life the fire of hope. Hope of deliverance, even in these direst of circumstances. To remind the people of the power of their God and the enduring promise of salvation. In their situation of ruin this means restoration. From a position of hopelessness they are called to move into a space in which hope can flourish. Such a movement is primarily mental and emotional. Even though, at present, there is no visible change on the horizon, the people are challenged to return to their hearts and to find there the consolation that will change the way that they assess and evaluate their situation. The prophet seeks to kindle in the hearts of the people a sense of deprivation that will, in turn, trigger a groundswell of desire.

Desire is a complex reality. It liberates us from the notion that the present can and should contain everything that will make us perfectly content. Desire is not far removed from discontentment. It is a subtle unwillingness to be satisfied by the range of delights that our present circumstances provide. In Victor Hugo's poem "Jeanne songeait," which I learned as a schoolboy many years ago, a young man is frantically trying to provide his girlfriend with everything that will make her happy. Is there anything else she wants? She raises her hand and points at *la lune immense*. She will not be happy until he gives her the moon. There is something a little unreasonable about genuine desire; it goes against common sense. It always seeks more than seems possible. The Latin verb *desiderare* has at its heart the root *sidera*, the stars; the prefix *de-* signals an absence. Desire is an impossible reaching out for the stars.

It is at the very heart of human nature to desire what it is unable to achieve. Probably the most famous sentence Saint Augustine wrote was, "You have made us for yourself and our hearts are restless until they rest in you." So many people hear this sentence once and remember it forever, because it says something about their intimate character that the purveyors of popular culture leave unsaid. It reminds us that we were made for infinity, for relationship with God; without it we will always be incomplete. And frustrated. We may seek substitutes and compensations, but they will never be enough. We will always desire more. And the irony is that we do not know what we desire. We know *that* we desire, but the object of our yearning surpasses our powers of expression.

What is meant by the promise of salvation is that God undertakes to give us that which we desire but cannot describe, much less achieve. We are delivered from existential despair by the gratuitous assurance that all will be well. When we speak about being saved, we are often more conscious of what we are saved from than of the gift which is given us. A gift beyond imagining. "Eye has not seen, nor ear heard, nor has it entered into the human heart to conceive what God has prepared for those who love him" (1 Cor 2:9). God delivers us from our present misfortunes by offering us something infinitely better. The first step is to put new heart into us. The situation is dark, and the prospect of improvement is minimal. If we can be led to accept that there will be, by the agency of God, a new dawning, then a glimmer of light appears in our hearts. By the hope thus aroused, the process of salvation has begun. As Saint Paul reminds us, it is in hope that we are saved (cf. Rom 8:24).

This hope—sustained by a firm confidence in God—is the source of the consolation that the prophet offers. God is determined to restore the remnant of his people to their homeland. But God's deliverance is larger than the repatriation of a few thousand exiles. It evokes a more universal promise. In the context of the Genesis narrative, all that was lost through Adam's sin will be recovered. There will be, indeed, a new heaven and a new earth—a new creation, what used to be termed "the brotherhood of man." In this process, we who are often in danger of being overwhelmed by the misery of our present condition will have a share. For the moment, however, we play a part by keeping alive our faith, our hope, and our desire. These are the sources of our consolation that the prophet seeks to encourage.

There is an obstacle to be surmounted: our habitual inertia. This can be more than the sluggishness of inaction. Inaction can take a paradoxical form. If we ever studied elementary physics we would know that inertia and momentum are merely different names for the same reality. Both bespeak a resistance to change. As we progress through life, we fashion for ourselves a manner of living that suits us, often by following the path of least resistance. We make sure that our little pleasures are included, and avoid as far as possible most of what irks us. There is no great malice in our harmless little lives, but the spirit of adventure has long ago passed away. In seeking to be moderate in everything, unaccountably we have become mediocre.[2] The last thing we want to face is an existential challenge. We want to stay as we are.

Prophets always challenge us, even though they do so under the overarching vault of God's mercy. They are not convinced by our benign press releases and our partisan interpretation of events. They say it as it is. The emperor has no clothes! They are not satisfied by our polite deceptions. They see through the webs of delusion that we create for ourselves. Their message is simple: have a change of heart and mind so that you can believe the good news. A message of change is the last thing we want to hear as we trolley along on our habitual tracks. We want to do only what we have always done. Even when life is hard and unfruitful we resist change; we fear that change will make things even worse.

This is true of most of us, at least in some areas of life. We want things to stay as sweet as they were. Even those who seem to be rabid for change have limits on their zeal. Vladimir Lenin preached radical revolution, yet insisted each day that his desk be cleared and that his books were returned exactly to their correct location on the shelves. No change in the ordering of his study was tolerated. Everything had to remain as it was. Those who interfered did so at their own peril. Mostly we limit our

---

[2] Thus, David Malouf, *A First Place* (North Sydney: Knopf, 2014), 301: "the preference for moderation easily leads to mediocrity."

desire for change to those areas that do not impinge on our own comfortable sameness. Unless we are comprehensively discontented with our lot, change is mostly for others.

If we can remember any occasions in our life in which we have embraced positive change, we will probably discover that we did so because someone we like and trusted urged us on. "Try this new food." "Come with me to the tennis match. I am sure you will enjoy it." "Let's have a holiday in Iceland; it's time we went somewhere different." We were surprised to find enjoyable possibilities outside the borders of our own previous experience. We just needed someone to invite us to make the leap. To accompany us both in deciding and in accomplishing. True friendship is always an invitation to keep growing, and this often involves changing.

To return to our existential inertia: How are we to overcome our reluctance to move beyond our present limits to a more abundant life? Mostly, this is done in company with others, and that points to the reality and the function of the church. We are initiated into this new life through the agency of others. But there is a deeper and more intimate level at which we are challenged to become more than we are. For this we need to have ongoing access to that source of consolation and strength without which any spiritual life falters. In other words, we need to set aside space and time in which we may give ourselves contact with the spiritual world. For most of us, this involves dedication to personal prayer.

Today we are surrounded by an abundance of electronic entertainment. For many it has become so addictive that they continue engaging with it long past their normal bedtime. As a result, it is said, many today are suffering from sleep deprivation and their well-being is in jeopardy. They feel tired, they are more irritable, there are more interpersonal difficulties, they are less efficient at work, and they have more traffic accidents. We need a regular quantum of sleep. Without it we become less human. Whatever advantages we believe we gain from our electronic engagements, their total effect often proves to be negative. In many cases, we don't know why things are not going well for us, because the effects of sleep deprivation are insidious. But they are real.

In the spiritual life, we can suffer from prayer deprivation. When religious people become prickly or grumpy or obsessed with trivia or demanding of others, it often signals that the interior flame has gone out and they are merely continuing to do the things that used to work but have long passed their expiry date. People do these things dutifully, but without much gratification, and with a lot of repressed resentment. They project onto others their own interior malaise, which tends to precipitate them into an endless cycle of antagonism and negativity. They develop an astonishing capacity to rationalize their situation so that others are always to blame, if not because of what they have done, then because of what they have not done. They turn their backs on the fact that is right in front of them. When they abandoned personal prayer, their lives began to disintegrate.

We sometimes find at least some traces of this in ourselves. If we permit ourselves to drift away from the regular practice of personal prayer, we will find that things slowly begin to fall apart. In particular, our ability to deal creatively with negative situations and unpleasant surprises is diminished. We find ourselves exiled from the spiritual life we once had. The solution is simple. We need to return to the practice we have discontinued. We need to return from the Babylon of our own making.

Why do we allow ourselves let the practice of regular prayer slip out of our lives? The first answer that comes to our minds is that there are so many other important and urgent things to be done that prayer is squeezed out. Or we claim that we need time to relax and unwind and this also begins to consume the minutes—perhaps hours. If we allowed ourselves to function, for a little while, as prosecutors, we would soon punch holes in these assertions. If we want to prove our blamelessness, we need to come up with a more convincing line of argument.

For most people, prayer becomes challenging as it changes. It tends to move beyond the heavily emotional uplift that lures beginners into its embrace and to become subtler, drawing the person into ever-more-profound stillness and peace. Yet within this peace, challenges lurk. The absence of pious entertainment gives rise to the possibility of a more comprehensive self-awareness—and this includes a stronger sense of desire for God coupled with a sober acknowledgment of the many liabilities that constrict its expansion. Saint John Climacus wrote, "Your prayer will soon show you in what state you are. Theologians say that prayer is the monk's mirror." The more we pray, the more we become aware of the precariousness of our virtue and of our need for the grace of God.

In 1967, C. Y. Glock and others published *To Comfort and to Challenge: A Dilemma of the Contemporary Church*.[3] The title points to a universal issue. Are churches to see themselves as comforting or as challenging? On which function is the most energy to be expended? The same problem confronted Second Isaiah. He wrote a book of comfort and consolation, yet many passages in it are confronting and challenging. The only possible conclusion is that there is comfort to be had, but only on the condition that the challenges are accepted. In our prayer, comfort and challenge go hand in hand. When the level of comfort seems to decline, it is usually because we are not facing the challenges that present themselves as our self-knowledge increases.

The comfort that we experience in prayer derives from our relationship with the person of Christ. As Saint Bernard of Clairvaux teaches, initially our meeting with Christ could almost be described as sentimental. Depending on temperament, there may be warmth of feeling, fervor, and enthusiasm. The presence of

---

[3] Charles Y. Glock, Benjamin B. Ringer, and Earl R. Babbie, *To Comfort and to Challenge: A Dilemma of the Contemporary Church* (Berkeley: University of California Press, 1967).

Christ is, for some, intrusive and, for a time, dominates their day. But this does not last. To facilitate growth in those who have made some progress, Christ ascends into heaven. "If we have known Christ Jesus according to the flesh, we know him thus no longer" (2 Cor 5:16). Yet he remains with them spiritually as a dear friend, a wise counselor, and a strong helper. The Lord is no longer to be sought where he was previously found. It is necessary to reach out to him with the arms of the spirit. There is still comfort to be found, but it is necessary for us to consent to the purifying work of the Holy Spirit in our souls, equipping us with the skills to find the One whom we seek. This usually means detachment. If we care to listen, we will hear a progressively stronger call to renunciation. We are summoned to leave aside everything that could become a substitute or a compensation for this deeper relationship to which we aspire. Christ says to us also, "If you will be perfect, renounce yourself and come, follow me." Not a message that most of us want to hear. When it is Christ who interiorly speaks thus to us, his invitation is wrapped in a sweetness that bespeaks its possibility. When it is merely the prompting of the superego, it triggers feelings of shame and guilt and self-belittlement. What Christ asks of us is habitually slight when compared with the subtle incentives that accompany his request. What our own perverted ambition for self-improvement demands is monstrously unrealistic.

There is always consolation to be had, even though the period during which we are reeducated so that we may perceive it is stern and unrelenting. By remaining with the negativity, struggling to be calm and still, we are assuaged from time to time with a ripple of peacefulness. This intimates to our newly sensitized heart that, in the end, all will be well.

Such periods of radical reorientation are obviously unavoidable. If, like Jonah, we try to run away from them, all that we will accomplish is postponement. We will run off in a loop and go on and on until we arrive back at the same place we were, maybe years afterward. Initiation into a more intimate form of prayer cannot be replaced by self-chosen good works. As the call comes, we need to respond. Even though our response will often be tepid, with God's help a momentum will slowly build up. But, as the Gospels admonish us, we need to keep on praying and not lose heart. When we become discouraged and cease investing energy in prayer, our practice either becomes a dreary routine or is abandoned altogether. We need to be obstinate and refuse to quit. Saint Gregory the Great reminds us that prayer is often better at the end than it was in the beginning. Even our clumsiest efforts eventually yield fruit.

Occasionally, it makes sense to conduct an audit of our practice of personal prayer. This is especially important for those who are professionally obliged to spend time in liturgy. Public prayer becomes part of their routine, and they may be tempted to say to themselves that they have done enough. The time we spend in personal prayer is our gift, and it is helpful to check that we are not shortchanging God. It is our contribution to the lifelong conversation between us and God. If we miss the opportunity to respond, the conversation is interrupted and contact is weakened. "Wherefore came I, and there was no man? I called, and none answered?" (Isa 50:2).

To review our practice we need to be practical. For myself, I consider four areas where there is often scope for recalibration. Have I a special place for prayer? Do I have a regular time for prayer? Do I allow for a buffer zone between prayer and my daily activities so that I arrive at prayer a little less distracted? Have I found a posture that enables me to sit quite still for the time I have allotted? Attention to these mundane and, perhaps, trivial elements helps me to build prayer into my daily life. They are not dramatic. They demand no special skills. They are not such as will lead to boastful self-importance. They are merely the first steps in the journey of a thousand miles. Anyone can take them. To keep myself motivated, I often call to mind the words written in the 1930s by Abbot John Chapman of Downside: "The only way to pray is to pray; and the way to pray well is to pray much. If one has no time for this, one must at least pray regularly. But the less one prays, the worse it goes."[4]

The practice of prayer teaches us how to pray. Or, rather, in coming to the aid of our feeble attempts to pray, the Holy Spirit becomes our instructor. "Prayer is God's gift to those who pray," says Saint John Climacus. We don't try to mastermind our journey into prayer nor attempt to control its progress. We simply give ourselves to practice and allow the Holy Spirit to bridge the vast abyss between us and the Father. The Holy Spirit is our advocate, our Paraclete, one named by John V. Taylor as "the Go-Between God."[5] This is not mere theology; we will also experience it for ourselves—especially if we are totally incompetent when it comes to prayer. Blessed are those who are inept at prayer, because they don't know enough to be able to interfere with the working of the Holy Spirit. Prayer is never the same, because it occurs at the intersection of our faith and the reality of our lives. As our lives change, so too does our prayer. Yesterday's prayer is no good; it has passed its expiry date. The only true prayer is that generated by the Holy Spirit today.

Some people make the mistake of striving too earnestly for "pure prayer." They read books, become enthused, and rush forward to take their place in the choir of angels. Prayer is simply a reaching out to God from wherever we happen to be. If we are tired or grumpy or overexcited, that has to be the point from which we begin. You may say that such a situation is not ideal. Certainly. But it is real, and reality has more of God in it than any ideal that we set for ourselves. We pray as we are, even though much in us cries out for redemption. We are what we are, and when we pray, we pray in as full awareness of what we are as we can manage. The first task for the exiles is to recognize that

---

[4] Dom Roger Hudleston, ed., *The Spiritual Letters of Dom John Chapman O.S.B.* (London: Sheed & Ward, 1923), 53.

[5] John V. Taylor, *The Go-Between God: The Holy Spirit and the Christian Mission* (London: SCM Press, 1972).

they are exiles. Further they need to acknowledge the fact of their own complicity in their misfortune and begin to see that their redemption can come only from God. It is from this starting point that prayer emerges.

Meanwhile, we are not single, isolated individuals. We are among those who share or have shared our predicament, and we can gain comfort and support from their presence. This usually means that we should not hesitate to populate our prayer—to invite others into our heart as we raise it to God. Especially as we begin our prayer. We include whatever concerns us at this moment. We carry it into the presence of God—friends, enemies, situations. And we do not have to go alone; Christian tradition encourages us to surround ourselves with "a cloud of witnesses," the saints and the angels and, especially, the Mother of Jesus. They are not so much the focus of our prayer or the object of our attention; they are more like the context out of which we pray. Even as our prayer becomes more free from overt content and moves toward becoming a "naked intent unto God," they remain with us because we are one in Christ. In some way, their prayer infuses ours with greater intensity. We are not alone. We draw strength from those who have gone before us.

Most of us live in a progressively secularized world that is not much less antipathetic to authentic religion than ancient Babylon. If we are to allow faith and hope to continue to exercise an influence over our lives, we must be ready to drink deeply from the fountain of consolation that the saints set before us. It was one of the mishaps of history that the immediate aftermath of the Second Vatican Council coincided with the rise of what was termed "secularization theology," the "death of God" movement. In the process of renewal, much was abandoned in the hope of creating a purer religion. As a result, many of the traditional forms by which devotion was expressed and fostered were discontinued. Even as early as 1969, Flemish theologian Edward Schillebeeckx characterized this process as a forcible ripping off of "the living skin of religious experience." Many of the faithful were left bereft of consolation, deprived of what alone can be an effective counterbalance to the attractions of a hedonistic and acquisitive society. And many simply gave up the practice of religion and, at best, settled for a vague, undemanding, and content-free "spirituality."

We need to discover new springs of devotion that will enable us to stand firm in our faith. Those of us who are not pure spirits will inevitably find that there is a feeling element in such devotion. It will not be the luscious fervor of our early days, but we will still feel a sense of uplift at the touch of God. We will taste and see for ourselves that the Lord is subtly sweet. A stillness descends on us, a peace that rises up within us to push aside the aggravations that may bedevil our daily existence. A transient whisper that, ultimately, all will be well.

There will be many challenges, but one of the most significant will be to overcome our reluctance to put ourselves in the way of meeting God. Faith without works is dead; faith without prayer is dying. We need to reinsert prayer so firmly into our ordinary daily schedules that it does not get washed away by the onrush of real and self-proclaimed urgencies. If we are lucky enough to live on Easy Street, with most of our needs met and our wishes granted, it may well be that we will tend to forget God, even though we make a slight effort to maintain some of the outward observances of religion. Good fortune does not last. The house built on sand does not stand. We need to develop habits that will serve us well in times of adversity.

Second Isaiah never dissimulated the hardship experienced by the exiled remnant of Israel. He understood the suffering and pain of an exiled and enslaved people. He also understood guilt and the shame that accompanied their realization of their own complicity in their downfall. The message he delivered, however, was one of hope, trusting in the power and fidelity of God. He offered them consolation, if only they would put themselves out, in order to lay hold of it. Because alienation from God was the root of all their woes, relief was to be found in turning once again to God. His exhortation to them, at the end of his book, is one to which we ourselves should listen:

> Seek the Lord while he may be found. Call on him while he is near. Let the wicked forsake their way and the evil their thoughts. Let them turn to the Lord and he will have mercy on them, and to our God for he will freely pardon. (Isa 55:6–7)

Do we really need any more admonition than that?

2

TRANSCENDENCE

Second Isaiah's "Book of Consolation" contains many surprises. One of the most unsettling is the amount of space the prophet devotes to parodying pagan worship of idols (cf. 40:19–20, 44:9–20, 45:20, 46:1–2, 46:5–7, 48:5). To us sophisticated moderns, the worship of manufactured images seems crass. Of all the commandments, we confidently assert, the prohibition against idolatry poses the least problem for us. Perhaps. The point that the prophet is making is that when we forsake the worship of the living God, we are compelled to find something to take its place. These substitutes are mostly stupid.

John Gray, himself an unbeliever, finds that many contemporary forms of atheism unconsciously seek to compensate for the absence of whatever it is that religions bring.[1] The purposes historically served by religion are left untouched by systems whose energy derives from mere denial. This is especially so when what is denied does not coincide with what religions assert. We do not have to be very knowledgeable about history to conclude that a world without God is not necessarily a paradise. While there are people of faith who contribute generously to the sum total of human misery, it is usually not because of their faith, but because of a fundamental distortion of the principles on which their religion is based.

---

[1] See John Gray, *Seven Types of Atheism* (London: Allen Lane, 2018).

In the postmodern situation, most unbelieving people are too mentally inert to be able to advance convincing arguments for the rejection of religion. The form that their unbelief takes is a practical atheism supplemented by a casual agnosticism. If they are broad-minded, they may tolerate religious belief and practice as an optional extra, like veganism or nudism. They say that others may choose to live thus, but they are not interested. Meanwhile, they refuse to have the preferences of adherents imposed on themselves. As for thinking through the position they have adopted, this is often left for others to do, or deposited into the "too hard" basket.

In a climate of burgeoning self-proclaimed "atheism," the question arises about how people are to respond to the occasional glimmers of a religious instinct that many experience. A common self-description of unbelievers is, "I am spiritual, but not religious." By this they seem to mean that they are somewhat aware of feelings that seem to derive from a sphere that is beyond that of the material, but they are disinclined to pursue the significance of what they have experienced through the medium of what established religions have to offer. These "intimations of immortality" remain outside a coherent system of meaning and, as such, have relatively little impact on daily life. They may prompt people to become lifelong seekers or religious dilettantes, but it is rare that they have any systematic influence on the choices by which everyday life is shaped.

Some people try to give substance to their spiritual feelings by adopting various practices, sometimes gathered under the umbrella of the New Age movement. At least some of them would probably incur Saint Paul's critique of being "zealous but without intelligence" (Rom 10:2). Practices are important, but persevering in them demands that they find a place within a system of meaning. Practice without theory slowly evaporates. In our supermarket culture, many like to pick and choose and end up with an eclectic mix of beliefs and practices that has no power to change lives. The Epistle to the Colossians speaks about *ethelothreskia*—self-made religion (2:23). It may be that we are not inclined to worship idols that are the work of our own hands, but sometimes we construct a religion that is not a response to the self-revelation of God but an unconscious expression of our own particular likes and dislikes. Perhaps disguised. As Saint Benedict writes, "What they agree with and like, they regard as holy; what they don't like, they regard as not allowed" (*Rule of Saint Benedict* 1:9). This is a much subtler form of idolatry than dancing around a golden calf or bowing to an idol made of wood.

The origins of authentic religion are not in this world of space and time. The journey toward a more spiritual life begins with an encounter with a numinous sacred that is not of this universe. It will not take the same form as Abraham being summoned from a safe existence in Ur of the Chaldees, or Jacob wrestling with an angel, or Moses puzzled by a burning bush. Our experience will not be like that of Isaiah or Jeremiah or Jonah. We will not hear a distinct call, as did Simon the fisherman and Matthew the tax gatherer. Yet there may well have been moments when, with the simplicity of a child, we found ourselves entranced by an inexplicable and invisible presence. A presence that was simultaneously awe-inspiring and friendly. We may not have had the vocabulary adequately to describe what we felt, yet the memory continues to color the sense of who we are. Perhaps, occasionally, we have been permitted to revisit this sacred encounter and to be energized by it or, maybe, it has just drifted away to become an evanescent memory.

What has happened is that, for a moment, we have stepped over the threshold into eternity. Ever so briefly, we have left behind the world of space and time and come into contact with a different reality. And we were subtly changed by the experience. Intuitively, we grasp that this spiritual sphere is not unconnected with the everyday world in which we live. There is a sense that, in some way, we are dependent on what we are, on this totally other universe, but we cannot fit it into any of the categories by which we usually make sense of our existence. For believers, the experience can be interpreted within the parameters of the faith system they have already accepted. For others, it remains a mystery that seeks a resolution, though with different degrees of urgency.

This experience is pointing to the existence of a transcendent reality outside the world of space and time but not unrelated to it. This reality is, in some way, accessible to us in moments of greater inner intensity. In a world in which idolatry was the norm, the prophet had to insist on the beyond-this-worldliness of the God whom the ancient forebears served. For us, the prophetic voice admonishes that there is more to life than what sense and intellect and bank managers can comprehend. We have to raise our eyes beyond the level of the mundane and to open our hearts to think deeper thoughts and to embrace a more comprehensive worldview:

> Know ye nothing? have ye not heard it? hath it not been told you from the beginning? have ye not understood it by the foundation of the earth? He sitteth upon the circle of the earth, and the inhabitants thereof are as grasshoppers, he stretcheth out the heavens as a curtain, and spreadeth them out, as a tent to dwell in. He bringeth the princes to nothing, and maketh the judges of the earth, as vanity, As though they were not planted, as though they were not sown, as though their stock took no root in the earth: for he did even blow upon them, and they withered, and the whirlwind will take them away as stubble. To whom now will ye liken me, that I should be like him, saith the Holy one? Lift up your eyes on high, and behold who hath created these things, and bringeth out their armies by number, and calleth them all by names: by the greatness of his power and mighty strength nothing faileth. (Isa 40:21–26)

Compared to God, the people are mere grasshoppers[2]—alive and kicking, important in their own sphere of existence, but as almost nothing compared to the Creator and Sustainer of the universe. Earth's inhabitants are no more than flies to be brushed away (51:6); Israel is like a worm (41:13). Whereas the Creator is eternal, the people are like grass, with no permanence; today they flower, tomorrow they wither and fade (40:6–8, 51:12). Compared to God, the people are deaf and blind (42:18), no better than drunks (51:21), yet stubborn and rebellious (48:4).

> Who hath measured the waters in his fist? and counted heaven with the span, and comprehended the dust of the earth in a measure? and weighed the mountains in a weight, and the hills in a balance? Who hath instructed the spirit of the Lord? or was his counselor, or taught him? Of whom took the counsel, and who instructed him and taught him in the way of judgment? or taught him knowledge, and showed unto him the way of understanding? Behold, the nations are as a drop of a bucket, and are counted as the dust of the balance: behold, he taketh away the isles as a little dust. And Lebanon is not sufficient for fire, nor the beasts thereof sufficient for a burnt offering. All nations before him are as nothing, and they are counted to him, less than nothing, and vanity. (Isa 40:12–17)

God's ways are inscrutable. Just as creation was a careful, measured act, so the providential flow of history is subject to God's governance. God has no need of human advice in this matter. Everything is under control:

---

[2] Oddly, Ezr 2:46 and Neh 7:48 mention the name of Hagab (or Hagabah), "grasshopper," among the temple attendants who returned from Babylon at the exile's end.

> Thus saith the Lord the King of Israel and his redeemer, the Lord of hosts, I am the first, and I am the last, and without me is there no God. And who is like me, that shall call and shall declare it, and set it in order before me, since I appointed the ancient people? and what is at hand, and what things are to come? let them show unto them. . . . All they that make an image, are vanity, and their delectable things shall nothing profit: and they are their own witnesses, that they see not nor know: therefore they shall be confounded. (Isa 44:6–7, 9)

God's eternity includes the total lordship of history. Outside space and time, God is subject to none of the limitations that dim the perceptions of those who dwell on earth. In other words, it is possible for God to foresee—and, thus, to describe in advance—what is going to happen. The prophet does this, in God's name, by pointing to Cyrus as the future conqueror of Babylon and the liberator of the people of Israel (45:1). Meanwhile, those who make and worship idols are doomed to futility:

> To whom will ye make me like, or make me equal, or compare me that I should be like him? They draw gold out of the bag, and weigh silver in the balance, and hire a goldsmith to make a god of it, and they bow down and worship it. They bear it upon the shoulders: they carry him and set him in his place: so doth he stand, and cannot remove from his place. Though one cry unto him, yet can he not answer, nor deliver him out of his tribulation. Remember this, and be ashamed: bring it again to mind, O you transgressors. Remember the former things of old: for I am God, and there is none other God, and there is nothing like me, Which declare the last thing from the beginning, and from of old: the things that were not done, saying, My counsel shall stand, and I will do whatsoever I will. I call a bird from the East, and the man of my counsel

> from far: as I have spoken, so will I bring it to pass: I have purposed it, and I will do it. (Isa 46:5–9)

The call to remembrance of past events is intended to evoke the memory of the exodus when, with a strong hand and an outstretched arm, the Lord led forth the people from the darkness of Egypt to the land of promise. The tribal memory of their ancient deliverance gives birth to the hope that God will do it again; once more to break down the iron gates that imprison the people and lead them forth on a smooth path through the desert to their own place:

> Hear me, O Jacob and Israel, my called, I am, I am the first, and I am the last. Surely mine hand hath laid the foundation of the earth, and my right hand hath spanned the heavens: when I call them, they stand up together. (Isa 48:12–13)

God acts through secondary agents, in this case Cyrus. They can do no other than follow God's instructions, even though they understand neither their source nor their ultimate meaning. The ways of God are beyond all human assessment. They are to be accepted and followed, even though their significance is enveloped by mystery.

> For my thoughts are not your thoughts, neither are your ways my ways, saith the Lord. For as the heavens are higher than the earth, so are my ways higher than your ways, and my thoughts above your thoughts. (Isa 55:8–9)

The God who was revealed to the Patriarchs and to Moses does not fit into any rational category. This God is One whose name cannot be pronounced. Not a comfortable god who can be conveniently fitted in with the prevailing social order, but One who disrupts what humans construct: who brings Abraham from

Ur and the children of Jacob from Egypt and now intends to bring back the pathetic remnant of Israel from the grip of all-powerful Babylon. A God beyond space and time and every human classification, yet continuing to exercise dominion over everything that happens on the earth:

> He bringeth the princes to nothing, and maketh the judges of the earth, as vanity, As though they were not planted, as though they were not sown, as though their stock took no root in the earth: for he did even blow upon them, and they withered, and the whirlwind will take them away as stubble. (Isa 40:23–24)

To elucidate the dialectic between the absence of God from this world and God's initial and ongoing agency in everything that happens in space and time, Second Isaiah has recourse to the notion of creation. We who begin to read the Bible with the first chapter of the Book of Genesis regard God's creation of the heavens and the earth as a teaching that has already been firmly established. But the matter is more complex. The idea of creation, evoked by synonyms such as "make" and "form," was known as early as Amos. Nevertheless, the specific verb used by Second Isaiah (*bara'*) certainly receives more emphasis in the Book of Consolation than anywhere else, even Genesis. It occurs seventeen times here, compared with eleven times in the Priestly narrative of Genesis. The form and pre-history of the word *bara'* are not altogether clear, but it seems to have gathered to itself its full range of connotations thanks to the creative genius of Second Isaiah.

The theological content of the theme indicates that, when God acts, there are no preconditions. God does not have to wait for a favorable time to intervene. "Behold, now is the favorable time" (2 Cor 6:2). Every time is appropriate for salvation. The Genesis account shows God's creative act overpowering the aggressive resistance of whatever was there before creation: *tohu wa-bohu*—a formless void that is antipathetic to any meaningful construct. A kind of cosmic black hole. Nothing, however, can stop the outpouring of God's creative act. Because there are no preconditions, there are no limits to what God can do. "Nothing is impossible for God." If God is the Creator, then God is also the Lord of history. Creation can be viewed as the first act in the history of salvation.[3]

God's creative activity reaches to the stars (Isa 40:26). This means that the heavenly bodies in all their splendor are created by God; to offer them worship is stupid. The sun and the moon are witnesses to the omnipotence of God. It is all-embracing, attaining even to the ends of the earth. It controls all space and time; past and future alike (41:20). God created humankind (45:12) and, specifically Israel (43:1), for a purpose (45:18), in order to manifest the divine radiance (43:7) and so to take the initiative in bringing about salvation and righteousness (45:8).

One of the most significant assertions about the Creator-God is found in an address to Cyrus, Israel's eventual liberator:

> I am the Lord, and there is none other; there is no God besides me: I girded thee, though thou hast not known me. That they may know from the rising of the sun, and from the West, that there is none besides me. I am the Lord, and there is none other. I form the light, and create darkness: I make peace, and create evil: I the Lord do all these things. (Isa 45:5–7)

This dense paragraph evokes many themes. By some, it is understood as a rejection of the dualistic system then emergent

---

[3] "A special feature in Deutero-Isaiah's thought about creation is, of course, that he does not regard creation as a work by itself, something additional to Yahweh's historical acts. Indeed, he seems to make no clear distinction here—for him creation is the first of Yahweh's miraculous historical acts and a remarkable witness of his will to save." Gerhard von Rad, *The Message of the Prophets* (London: SCM Press, 1973), 208.

in the Persian religion that is associated with the name of Zarathustra. The universe is not the battleground of two opposing forces—good and evil—with the outcome by no means certain. Everything that exists—whether we label it good or evil—comes from the creative hand of God. This means that everything that happens falls within the scope of divine providence. In ways that we do not and cannot understand, all things work together unto good—even the sin of Adam and Eve; the defeat by Nebuchadrezzar,[4] the defilement of the Temple, the deportation to Babylon, the desolation, and the despair. All these disasters ultimately are from God—to achieve benefits that are mostly beyond human understanding.

The exiles must have been like Job, sitting in the rubbish dump and wondering why so many troubles have befallen him, convinced of his own righteousness and seeing no cause for the effects that had devastated his otherwise happy life. The answer given to Job by God is similar to that which Second Isaiah formulates. God transcends human rationality. We have no right to demand explanations for what God has done or allowed to happen. We have to draw from our previous experience of the ways of God, the assurance that nothing happens beyond God's designing. Even though sometimes life is difficult, even impossible, it does not mean that God has deserted us. Sometimes it means that we have deserted God, but more often it is simply God working through secondary agencies to produce an ultimately beneficial outcome. That is probably why we are frequently admonished not to allow our resentments at wrongs done to us to shape our lives. Our persecutors are unknowingly doing the work of God:

> Who among you shall hearken to this, and take heed, and hear for afterwards? Who gave Jacob for a spoil,

---

[4] I am adopting the more correct spelling, often attested in the Book of Jeremiah.

> and Israel to the robbers? Did not the Lord, because we have sinned against him? for they would not walk in his ways, neither be obedient unto his Law. Therefore he hath poured upon him his fierce wrath, and the strength of battle; and it set him on fire round about, and he knew not, and it burned him up, yet he considered not. (Isa 42:23–25)

Disaster is intended to break open the hard shell of complacency that shielded the people from the recognition of their real dependence on God. At different times and in various ways, God admonished them through the prophets, but the warning went unheeded. A more drastic intervention became necessary. Second Isaiah is encouraging the exiles to see in their desolation a call to recognize the reality that, of themselves, they are helpless, but with God, a good result may yet accrue. Not a message any of us want to hear, but when life goes awry, it helps the seeds of hope to germinate.

It is because God exists beyond the reach of material influences that nothing happening in the world of space and time can affect what God proposes to do. Present reverses in the fortunes of God's people do not necessarily point to a powerlessness in God; they are more like a strategic withdrawal in order to strike more fiercely at opposing forces, giving Israel the possibility of finally coming to its senses. God takes seriously the role of redeemer or avenger, *go'el*. Second Isaiah uses this title for God nine times. Its meaning may have been weakened by its use as a conventional epithet, but it retains some sense of positive intervention in favor of someone, whether this be a matter of wreaking vengeance, or paying ransom money, or restoration to a former status. God will not forever stand idly by when Israel is captive. The time will come when a divine intervention will effect a change in fortune. Second Isaiah's message is that this time of redemption is fast approaching. "In the time of my favor I will answer you. In the day of salvation I will help you" (49:8).

The transcendence of God does not mean that God is uninterested in what transpires on earth. It means only that God is not influenced or constrained by what happens here. This will later be affirmed as the doctrine of divine immutability. The good news for us is that there is no failure of ours that will cause God to abandon plans of redemption and salvation. These will go ahead, but in God's time and not ours and according to the modalities of Providence, which are so often beyond our powers of comprehension:

> Can a woman forget her child, and not have compassion on the son of her womb? though they should forget, yet will I not forget thee. Behold, I have graven thee upon the palm of mine hands: thy walls are ever in my sight. (Isa 49:15–16)

> Is mine hand so shortened, that it cannot help? or have I no power to deliver? (Isa 50:2)

Associated with this proclamation of God as the transcendent Creator of all is the assertion that there is no other God but the God of Israel. Only God is God. Second Isaiah insists on a strictly monotheistic faith whereas previously there may have been traces of henotheism (adherence to one deity among many). The God of Israel was seen as the supreme and only God, and not merely one that is greater than all the other gods. The prophet will accept nothing of this. The Lord Our God is alone. Other claimants to divinity are false because they are powerless. Powerless to change things. Powerless to predict what will happen. Powerless to save those stupid enough to believe in them.

Since there is only one God, the God of Israel is also the God of all nations. This means that the divine favors are not limited to Israel or to the remnant of Israel, but will be poured out on peoples of all nations. Within this universalist perspective, Israel has a mission. As the recipient of the divine self-revelation, it is to serve as the channel by which the truth of God is to be manifested to the Gentiles. Israel is to be a "covenant for the people" (42:6, 49:8) sent to bring the light of *mishpat*, the rule of divine righteousness, to the Gentiles (42:1, 6). This vision of a unified humanity under God finds even stronger expression in the final chapters of Third Isaiah.

Because of this future mission of evangelization the humbled survivors of Israel are to be kept alive, so that, eventually, a faithful remnant may be sufficiently restored to exercise its destined role of influence in bringing the reign of God closer to reality. If the exiles can be convinced of the need for them to remain mindful of their mission, then glimmers of hope will not be entirely extinguished.

The basis for all hope is the acceptance that we are part of God's plan for the universe, and because God is beyond the influence of any constraints coming from the sphere of space and time, this plan is certain and irrevocable. The transcendence of God is the ground of our hope. If, in the act of creation, God is able to make something out of nothing, then the hopelessness of our present situation cannot be an obstacle to God's saving action. Because hope is proportioned to the competence of the one on whose help we are relying, theological hope is not limited. It takes its character from the infinitude of God.[5] Whether consciously done or not, to reduce God to human scale is to subvert the dynamism of hope:

> Knowest thou not or hast thou not heard, that the everlasting God the Lord, hath created the ends of the earth? He neither fainteth, nor is weary; there is no searching of his understanding. But he giveth strength unto him that

---

[5] Thomas Aquinas, *Summa Theologiae* II-II, 18, 4 ad 2: "Hope does not depend mainly on grace already possessed but on the divine omnipotence and mercy, by which one who does not have grace can obtain it, and thus come to eternal life."

> fainteth and unto him that has no strength he increaseth power. Even young men shall faint and be weary and the young men shall stumble and fall, But they that wait upon the Lord will renew their strength; they shall lift up the wings as the eagles; they shall run and not be weary; and they shall walk and not faint. (Isa 40:28–31)

Second Isaiah's teaching about the divine transcendence is not something that alienates us from God, causing us to keep a safe distance. Rather it is a spur to confidence. Here is a source of help in even the direst of disasters "for nothing is impossible for God." This certainty is doubled when we consider that God is aggressively on our side, our *go'el*, our Avenger, our Redeemer, our Restorer—even though we don't fully understand how what has happened in the past and what is happening right now will contribute to a glorious conclusion.

3

SERVANTHOOD

God's plan to bring humanity to salvation was to be accomplished through the active participation of secondary agents. This meant that those chosen for a task had to be equipped with the necessary insight, skill, zeal, and endurance to be able to fulfill their mission. Such a person was designated as God's servant. In the Old Testament the verb *'abad* and the noun *'ebed* and their cognates occur over one thousand times in a variety of contexts.[1] Inevitably such a common term as "service" ranges over a wide spectrum of meanings. It can refer to different types of work, the performance of an office, the state of lifelong attachment to a master, and various degrees of servitude including slavery. However, the term can have honorific connotations. For example, the "servants" of the king may be more than domestic attendants: they may also fulfill a role similar to what is expected of "ministers" in the Westminster system of governance. They may serve as emissaries and counselors. The concept is also applied to those who serve God through their participation in the official worship of the Temple.

Second Isaiah uses the full title *'ebed YHWH*, servant of YHWH, only in 42:14; elsewhere the relationship with God is signified by a possessive pronoun. The expression does not

[1] The Septuagint rendered the word for "servant" about equally by *doulos* and *pais*.

simply designate an ordinary worshipper of Israel's God. We know this because it was also applied to the Patriarchs, and to such figures as Moses and David. The term "servant" implies a special relationship resulting from the divine election. These men were specially chosen by God to be the mediators of God's self-revelation. They enjoyed a closeness to God that was not granted to others. Whereas God spoke to the prophets by visions, he spoke directly to Moses, face-to-face (Exod 33:11; Num 12:7–8). Something similar is true of the Patriarchs, who enjoyed immediate encounters with God. To be God's servant was a special honor, since it involved receiving a mandate to perform a special service in bringing about the realization of God's plans. Thus, Jeremiah gives the title to Nebuchadrezzar, as an instrument of God's retribution (Jer 25:9, 27:6, 43:10), and Second Isaiah calls Cyrus "servant" because of his role in reversing Israel's fortunes. The prophets are also referred to as God's servants, usually collectively, although Second Isaiah never uses the word *nabi'* (prophet) or any of its cognates. Prophets have a role of speaking in the name of God and reminding the people of their obligations under the covenant. Again, the emphasis is on their relationship with God; whatever task they are called to perform is accomplished by virtue of this relationship. If there is no real relationship with God, the person must be considered a false prophet, irrespective of whether their words are true or false.

The theme of the servant is especially strong in Second Isaiah. Most people are familiar with the Servant Songs and their application to Christ. It is probably prudent, however, not to be too quick in making this identification, since the theme is a complex tapestry whose many threads often seem discordant. Sometimes the servant is named; sometimes he is anonymous. Sometimes the servant is Israel; at other times the servant is one who is sent on a mission to Israel. In some texts, the reference is clearly to a concrete individual; in others, it seems more abstract, referring perhaps to a corporate personality. It is probably best to accept that the notion of servanthood is a fluid one. Maybe this is because several authors contributed to the final product. Maybe it is because the author was not a systematic thinker, approaching his topic intuitively from different angles, and not bothering to reshape his material according to the demands of sequential logic. Here, as elsewhere in the Scriptures, we must be content to follow the text as we meander through the book, recognizing that the intellectual world from which it comes was different from that which we inhabit. It is an abuse to attempt to manipulate the text so that it corresponds to our way of thinking. We are the ones who need to change. We need to step out of the self-assured, categorized world we inhabit and open ourselves both to what is expressed and to what is left unexpressed in this ancient text that we are considering. As hard as it is for us to admit, we have to concede that, with regard to the many questions raised by Second Isaiah's treatment of the theme of servanthood, "no conclusive resolution seems possible at this time."[2]

Servanthood must be viewed as a privilege rather than an imposed burden. God takes the initiative and breaks into human self-sufficiency by calling one who has been chosen. The verb *qara'* is used in several overlapping senses by Second Isaiah. A call creates the beginning or the activation of a relationship. We cry out in order to attract attention. We add a positive hue to this opening gambit by addressing someone by name. We call someone to participate in a task we have envisaged, thus the relationship is given concrete expression as well as some degree of permanence. All of these meanings are contained in the various texts where it is said that God calls or summons his servant.

---

[2] Helmer Ringgren, s.v. "*'abad*," in *Theological Dictionary of the Old Testament*, vol. 10 (Grand Rapids: Eerdmans, 2003), 403. See also Childs, *Introduction*, 334: "The picture of the servant of Yahweh is so divergent that the majority of scholars feel constrained to speak of two different figures under the same image. On the one hand, the servant is viewed as collective Israel; on the other, he is an individual."

The call is not unpremeditated. The servant has been chosen by a deliberate act, although the reason for being called is not always apparent to the one who receives the summons. God's choices rarely conform to human expectations:

> God has chosen the foolish of the world to shame the wise. God has chosen the weak of the world to shame the strong. God has chosen common folk with no status, those who are nothing, to bring to nothing those who are something. (1 Cor 1:27–28)

God's choice of Israel does not imply a rejection of those outside the chosen nation, a legitimation of exceptionalism. Israel's role is to be an instrument of inclusion for all nations. This is one aspect of Second Isaiah's vision. Israel is to serve the purpose of a more universal salvation. The result of God's choice is not a privilege but a mission. Furthermore, the working of the divine election does not presuppose any preexisting quality in those chosen (cf. Deut 7:7–8). God's choice creates worthiness. A call from God is a summons to become great; it is the beginning of the process and not its end. We see this also in Jesus's choice of the first Apostles, who grew from their nondescript backgrounds to become the pillars of the church, ready to defy the empire rather than to desist from their mission. The call of Israel and of those chosen for special roles within it contained within itself the creative power of God to make something out of nothing, to support and sustain what was created, and to bring to nothing those who intended to wreak destruction upon what had been brought into being with such infinite forethought:

> But thou, Israel, art my servant, and thou Jacob, whom I have chosen, the seed of Abraham my friend. For I have taken thee from the ends of the earth, and I called thee before the chief thereof and said unto thee, "Thou art my servant." I have chosen thee and not cast thee away.

> Fear thou not, for I am with thee. Be not afraid, for I am thy God. I will strengthen thee, and help thee and will sustain thee with the right hand of my justice. Behold, all they that provoke thee shall be ashamed and confounded; those who oppose thee will be as nothing, and they that strive with thee shall perish. Thou shall seek them and shalt not find them, to wit the men of thy strife they shall be as nothing and the man that war against thee, as a thing of naught. For I the Lord, thy God, will hold thy right hand and saying unto thee, Fear not, I will help thee. Fear not thou worm Jacob and ye men of Israel, I will help thee, saith the Lord and thy redeemer, the holy one of Israel. (Isa 41:8–14)

This is a strong text that demonstrates that Israel's servanthood involves much more than being associated with a particular task. The title bespeaks a profoundly interpersonal relationship. This relationship persists even though Israel is conscious of past infidelity and its present degradation to the extent that it can make its own the words of the Psalmist, "I am a worm, not a man" (Ps 22:60). "In the context of exile, when Israel feels itself like a worm and has grounds for seeing itself cast off by Yahweh because of its waywardness, Yahweh assures it that it actually has the exalted status Jacob and David had as Yahweh's chosen servant. Yahweh has not rejected it."[3] Israel is addressed as the "seed" of Abraham; this is a powerful expression when it is remembered that it was believed that semen contained the whole of a person's genetic coding, handed on through the male line from generation to generation and to be preserved at all cost. What Abraham was, Israel as his descendant is. Just as Abraham was considered a friend of God, so is Israel: chosen, called, strengthened, and sustained.

---

[3] John Goldingay, "Servant of Yahweh," in *Dictionary of the Old Testament Prophets*, Mark J. Boda and J. Gordon McConville, eds. (Nottingham: InterVarsity Press, 2012), 701.

Another text, however, includes Sarah in this honorable lineage. "Look to the rock from which you were cut and to the quarry from which you were hewn. Look to Abraham, your father, and to Sarah who gave you birth" (Isa 51:1–2).

The protection afforded to the descendants of Abraham is neither passive nor merely defensive. The divine transcendence means that those who strive against God will necessarily be foiled. The word *go'el* (used nine times in Second Isaiah) suggests that God is the avenger, the liberator, the ransomer, or the redeemer of his people. Those who now wage war against Israel will, in the future, be brought to nothing. The present misfortune is not denied, but a different future is foretold. This is why Israel is admonished, "Do not be afraid" (41:10, 41:13, 43:1, 51:7). The principal enemy to be overcome is not the might of the Babylonian Empire but a failure of confidence in the divine promises. The work is God's; Israel's task is to have total confidence in the reality of its vocation and to resist any temptation to abandon it in the face of pressing difficulties:

> But now, saith the Lord that created thee, O Jacob, and he that formed thee, O Israel: Fear not, for I have redeemed thee; I have called thee by thy name; thou art mine. When thou passeth through the waters I will be with thee; and through the floods, that they do not overflow thee. When thou walketh through the very fire, thou shalt not be burnt, neither shall the flame kindle upon thee. For I am the Lord, thy God, the holy one of Israel, thy Saviour; I gave Egypt for thy ransom, Ethiopia and Seba for thee. Because thou wast precious in my sight and thou wast honorable, and I loved thee, therefore will I give man for thee, and people for thy sake. Fear not, for I am with thee. (Isa 43:1–5)

God's continuing relationship with his people is a reason for their assurance of safety and for their liberation from the burden of fear. On the one hand, Israel is God's special or treasured possession (cf. Exod 19:5) to be protected from damage or loss. On the other hand, God accompanies his people through all the dangers they encounter on their journey. Floods cannot sweep them away. Fires cannot consume them. To be God's servant is to be more than a servant. It means being bound to God by the unbreakable bond of the covenant: "I will be your God. You will be my people." By a free choice, God is as much indentured to maintain the relationship as Israel. The connection is permanent.

The God of Israel is a God who delivers the chosen people from bondage. But a further step must be taken. The servants of the God of Israel must realize that they are called to be agents of divine liberation as well as recipients. They are called to participate in God's saving work. And their task is global. None can be truly free until all are free.

To be a servant, therefore, is to be entrusted with a mission, to be the human agency by which God's saving work is accomplished. "I will make you into a threshing-board—new and sharp with many teeth. You will thresh the mountains and crush them, reducing the hills to chaff" (Isa 41:15). The agricultural allusions may be a little unclear to us, but there is a manifest reminder that there is vigorous work to be done, despite Israel's puniness. As was stated in the opening verses of Second Isaiah, whatever is an obstacle to God's saving work must be energetically eliminated: mountains and hills laid low and rugged terrain leveled. And the servant of God has a role to play in this process. The identification and elimination of obstacles are tasks requiring a great deal of discernment, as well as practical insight and skillful tactics. Building a highway for the Lord requires a certain expertise to ensure that the energy expended is not wasted. More than brute force is involved. It must be guided by a keen intelligence that is able to perceive the hidden underpinnings of all human endeavors.

The vigorous identification and destruction of impediments, however, is only a first stage. Beyond this, God's servant is "called to establish the rule of God's law [*mishpat*] among the Gentiles" (42:1–3); "to be a covenant for the people and a light for the Gentiles" (42:6); "to open eyes that are blind, to free captives from prison, and to release from the dungeon those who sit in darkness" (42:7); to bring Jacob back to God (49:5); to restore the tribes of Jacob (49:6); to be a light for the gentiles so as to extend God's salvation to the ends of the earth (49:6); to heal (53:5); and to offer justification to a great multitude (53:11).

Such a comprehensive mission is clearly beyond the capacity of the poor worm, Israel. Such a glorious outcome can be the result only of God's working. And yet Israel is called to play a significant and even necessary part in the fulfillment of God's plan. This will necessarily involve a great cost to itself. The servant is not the master, but one who does what is bidden by another and sometimes, at least, has no understanding of the ultimate meaning of the work that has been assigned or how its personal contribution finds a place in the grand scheme of cosmic events:

> Hear, ye deaf and ye blind, regard that ye may see. Who is blind but my servant? Or deaf as my messenger that I sent? Who is blind as the [one who has my trust] and blind as the Lord's servant? Seeing many things but thou keepest them not. Opening the ears, but he heareth not. (Isa 42:18–19)

There is no scope for self-exaltation in the servant's role. True servants of God will always be prone to experiencing the "imposter syndrome." They do not feel responsible for the beneficent effects resulting from their meager performance. They consider themselves unprofitable servants and are amazed at the consequences of what they have done. The principle is clearly stated by Saint Paul: "I planted. Apollos watered. But it was God who gave the increase" (1 Cor 3:6). This requires of God's servants the humility to act as conduits of the divine power, restraining themselves so as not to leave their grubby fingermarks on the outcome. "We have this treasure in pottery vessels so that the abundance of power may [be seen to] belong to God and not come from ourselves" (2 Cor 4:7). The servant must be ready to decrease so that Christ may increase. This attitude is decidedly countercultural in a period in which self-assertion is valued. The willingness to step back and to make room for others is not always regarded as a precious disposition, but when it comes to cooperating with God, it is unqualifiedly essential.

If it is challenging to allow God to act through us, it is even more challenging to allow God to remain inactive—to accept that Providence may judge it wiser to defer the fruition of our labor. Because of separation in space or time, we may not live to see the outcome of our investment. Here the principle is, "One sows. Another reaps" (John 4:37). This rule is true regarding missionary activity; it is also true in the life of prayer. We have the word of Jesus that our prayer will certainly yield results, but more often than not the results that we envisaged, at the time for which we had been hoping, do not emerge. To our enfeebled mind, it seems that our prayer has been ineffectual. "One sows. Another reaps." The servant is expected to continue working at the assigned task even when it has begun to seem meaningless. It is not the servant who decides about the value of a particular operation; this is the master's prerogative. The servant's role is to be at the service of the master's directives.

The lack of visible results may well lead God's servant to exclaim, "I have labored in vain and spent my strength with no result and for nothing" (Isa 49:4). Discouragement is a persistent temptation for all who give themselves to God's service. Because there is no direct causal link between their expenditure of energy and visible outcomes, there is always a lurking suspicion that they are wasting their time. To make things worse, those around them may judge by externals and reinforce the impression of futility. As a result, God's servants can often find themselves without much social support in their labors. Worse, they may find themselves the objects of reprobation, facing not only indifference but active hostility. Survival in such circumstances is dependent on constant activation of the relationship with God. When human support is denied, recourse must be made to a higher agency:

> I gave my back unto the smiters and my cheeks to the nippers; I hid not my face from shame and spitting. For the Lord God will help me, therefore shall I not be confounded: therefore have I set my face like a flint, and I know that I shall not be ashamed. He is near that justifieth me: who will contend with me? Let us stand together: who is mine adversary? Let him come near to me. Behold the Lord God will help me: who is he that condemn me? Lo, they shall all wax old like a garment: the moth shall eat them up. Who is among you that feareth the Lord? Let him hear the voice of his servant: he that walketh in darkness, and hath no light, let him trust in the name of the Lord, and stay upon his God. (Isa 50:6–10)

A large part of discouragement is due to having lost contact with the source of encouragement. We become disheartened when we allow ourselves to drift away from God, when we lose contact with spiritual world, when the work we do takes precedence over our relationship with God. We begin to act as autonomous agents. We cease to be channels of divine intervention, and eventually things go awry. That is when discouragement sets in. To avoid this downward spiral, we need to keep open our channels of communication with God. In our efforts to be faith-filled servants of God we need to remember the principle: Faith without works is dead; faith without prayer is dying. When our best efforts yield no result beyond the eloquent disapproval of others, we need to set our faces like flint and place our hopes in God.

This reliance on God is most starkly described in the fourth and most famous of the Servant Songs. It is worthwhile reflecting on this significant text (52:13–53:12) at some length. The passage is not without obscurity. In part this is due to the profundity of its message. The language itself is both allusive and elusive and sends some commentators scurrying to find a plausible meaning. Here, as elsewhere, it is probably better to pay more attention to the tidal movement of the text, rather than to be distracted by over-concern with its puzzling details, which may well be the result of a complicated history of transmission:

> Behold my servant shall prosper: he shall be exalted and extolled, and be very high. As many were astonished at thee—his visage was so deformed of men and his form of the sons of men, so shall he sprinkle many nations. The kings shall shut their mouths at him; for that which had not been told them shall they see, and that which they had not heard shall they understand. (Isa 52:13–14)

The song begins with an evocation of the stark contrast between the servant's glorious future and his present state. Shockingly, the servant appears as no longer human; even the normally articulate are speechless at the sight. The reference to sprinkling is very obscure; some commentators dodge it by amending the text. Mostly the verb is used in a ritual context that seems out of place in the present context. Maybe it somehow indicates that many nations will be dumbfounded at what is happening before their eyes. The passage strongly affirms the discontinuity between the present distress of the servant and the bliss to be experienced following the intervention of God. This is a principle that we all have to bear in mind when things go against us. The chaos produced by deficient human activity will be transformed into something very good by the creative hand of God. There is no scope for despair; faith in the God of Israel has within itself a solid component of hope. This is the thesis: the future exaltation of God's servant is in no way jeopardized by his present state of degradation or by the rejection that he experiences:

> Who will believe our report? And to whom is the arm of the Lord revealed? But he shall grow up before him as a branch, and as a root out of a dry ground. He hath neither form nor beauty. When we shall see him, there shall be no form that we should desire him. He is despised and rejected of men. He is a man full of sorrows and hath experience of infirmities. We hid as it were our faces from him: he has despised and we esteemed him not. (Isa 53:1–3)

The promise of a glorious outcome seems beyond belief, so desperate is the servant's situation. There is nothing presently visible that would ground any hope of positive change. The ground is dry, but yet a seedling sprouts. But the new plant is not unaffected by its harsh environment. It emerges stunted and wilting, without the fresh candor we associate with new growth. The servant's extreme suffering does not provoke sympathy, but deepens the observer's disgust. This is a point worth pondering. There is total alienation from a potentially supportive community, as if the servant were guilty of some heinous crime. Thus, applying the verse to the exiles, even the horrors of devastation and deportation suffered following the Babylonian victory may well seem to be grounds not for compassion but for contempt. It is as though Israel deserved its fate. We may, perhaps, think of Job, not only subjected to unbelievable suffering but denied any genuine comfort by those he had considered his friends. And not only that; he was mocked and rebuked by them for failing to recognize something of which they were certain: his complicity in his own misfortune. Perhaps this will always be the lot of those whose confidence rests so entirely with God that they do not rely on human help. Their trust in God is viewed correctly as a rejection of the self-proclaimed omnipotence of human society. Here, as elsewhere, appearances are deceptive. The suffering of God's servants and prophets is not weakness but a subtle strength, one that, by its endurance, mutely calls out to the *go'el* for radical intervention:

> Surely he hath borne our infirmities and carried our sorrows. Yet we did judge him as plagued and smitten of God, and humbled. But he was wounded for our transgressions; he was broken for our iniquities. The chastisement of our peace was upon him and with his stripes we are healed. (Isa 53:4–5)

This section introduces an unanticipated element: the sufferings of God's servant are in some way vicarious. Second Isaiah invites his readers to own their complicity not only in the harsh treatment accorded God's servant, but also in the rejection of him as one accursed by God. We meet here some of the rich complexity associated with the notion of corporate personality. Israel is both the afflicted servant and those who distance themselves from him, simultaneously the sinner and the one unjustifiably suffering the effects of sin. The servant pays a price, and others reap the benefits. Here is a great paradox: the wounds inflicted on the servant are the means by which our wounds are healed. To view matters from a different angle: the misery we experience somehow reduces the misery experienced by others. It is as though we, as God's servants, are called upon to pay the debt that others have incurred. And, so, we are simultaneously those justly punished and those gratuitously acquitted. *Simul peccator et iustus.*

> All we like sheep have gone astray; we have turned everyone to his own way, and the Lord hath laid upon him the iniquity of us all. He was oppressed and he was afflicted, yet he did not open his mouth. He is brought as a sheep to the slaughter, and as a sheep before her shearer is dumb, so he openeth not his mouth. (Isa 53:6–7)

To comprehend the meaning of suffering and death, we need to have a profound awareness of our own sinfulness. Refusing to appreciate our complicity in evil launches us into an endless cycle of denial. Just as Adam blamed Eve for his disobedience and Eve blamed the serpent, so their descendants continue to look outside themselves for the sources of their troubles. Sin is defiance of God's life-giving and creative word. It results in the diminishment of life, expressed symbolically in the Bible through several metaphorical streams including illness, uncleanness, the sense of being lost, and the state of interior oppression or guilt.[4] By inhibiting our vitality, sin increases the power of a gradual death, which will continue to thwart our efforts at a fuller life, not only for ourselves but for those around us and for humanity as a whole. We have all made our contribution to the miserable plight of humankind. Things can improve only after we recognize this. The unraveling of the constrictive coils of sin begins with self-knowledge, whereby the life-denying effects of bad choices become apparent and the opportunity to reverse course is perceived and taken. Individual Israelites recognize that it is through their own evil lives that Israel as God's servant has been brought to nothing. It is a moment of deep compunction and astringent grief. Innocent Israel has been betrayed by its own people, for they have defied God and cut themselves off from the source of salvation:

> He was taken out from prison, and from judgement: and who shall declare his age? For he was cut out of the land of the living; for the transgressions of my people was he plagued. And he made his grave with the wicked and with the rich in his death, though he had done no wickedness, neither was any deceit in his mouth. (Isa 53:8–9)

Israel as an idealized corporate entity had committed no fault; the damage was done by individuals. Not in a single, dramatic moment but through a lifetime of undramatic infidelity to God's call and invitation. Omission. The cumulative effect of the sins of many was the annihilation of Israel. The decline was both

---

[4] We explore this theme more fully in a later chapter.

gradual and sudden. Not by unanticipated violence but by the slow processes of forensic justice. Israel was examined and found guilty and given over to punishment. "For the transgressions of my people was he plagued." We see here how Second Isaiah alternates between corporate and individual: between the Servant, as the idealized and fulfilled Israel, and the mass of sinful Israelites. Perhaps the poet saw the life of Israel encapsulated in the life of a single individual, perhaps not. In any case, the life of the whole is expressed through the living parts, and what happens in the parts has an effect on the health and welfare of the whole. The interchange between Israel and Israelites is described in terms similar to those Saint Paul used to characterize the reciprocal relationship between the body and its members: "For if one died for the sake of all, then all have died" (2 Cor 5:14). The fate of the community of Israel is inseparable from that of its members. If one is distressed, all are afflicted. The sin of one reduces the vitality of all. The Servant is dead and buried through no fault of his own: "He had done no wickedness, neither was any deceit in his mouth."

> Yet the Lord would break him and make him subject to infirmities: when he shall make his soul an offering for sin, he shall see his seed and shall prolong his days and the will of the Lord shall prosper in his hand. He shall see of the travail of his soul and shall be satisfied: by his knowledge shall my righteous servant justify many, for he shall bear their iniquities. (Isa 53:10–11)

The sacrifice of the servant is not without purpose. Second Isaiah finds meaning in the suffering inflicted on the Servant by viewing him in terms of a sacrificial victim that must be completely annihilated so that the sin-offering may be effective. When, by his death, the Servant negates the power of sin, then Israel is free of its encumbrance and so comes alive. Although put to death and buried, the Servant may look forward to a long life and numerous offspring. The Servant has completed his task as the agent of God's salvation and so is able to appreciate that, in some mysterious way, his suffering has been the means by which the many have been made righteous, because he has carried away their iniquities:

> Therefore will I give him a portion with the great, and he shall divide the spoil with the strong, because he hath poured out his soul unto death, and he was counted with the transgressors and he bore the sins of many and prayed for their trespasses. (Isa 53:12)

The exaltation of the Servant, trumpeted at the beginning of the song, is realized. Although put to death, he is still alive and enjoying the spoils of victory. Although he was previously regarded as a criminal, now his quality is celebrated. The Servant's victory is not, however, for himself alone. It has benefits for the many. Through his intercessory act, their sins are carried away.

It is highly improbable that the Christian reader will be able to meditate on this fourth Servant Song without thinking of the manner in which the death of Jesus is narrated in the New Testament. In the 1985 edition of *The Greek New Testament*, there are seven citations and thirty-four other references to this relatively short text, occurring in all four Gospels and in eight other New Testament books. There seems to be no doubt that the New Testament writers found in it a key to understanding the meaning of Jesus's death; it was undeserved, it yielded fruit for the many and it ended in glorification. Here we have the key elements for a theology of the paschal mystery, not only as it applies to Christ, but also as a way of understanding the life experiences of every fervent Christian.

It is prudent not to make of Second Isaiah one who predicted in detail the future sufferings of Jesus. He was, rather, formulating a revolutionary principle that envisaged innocent suffering as being, in some paradoxical way, redemptive for others. He was attempting to find an answer to the universal puzzlement generated when bad things happen to good people. His response was that all that happens comes ultimately from the hand of God, which accomplishes its beneficent purposes by ways that we are unable to comprehend. The Evangelists and others appreciated this teaching and allowed it to influence their way of narrating the passion and death of Jesus.

The fourth Servant Song gives us the most profound picture of how the life of a perfect servant of God unfolds. The proclamation of suffering as part of servanthood is not, however, to be understood as an invitation to masochism. Suffering is only half of the totality. The other half is the grace given to endure the affliction and, in some undefined way, to experience it not as punitive but as purgative. If we become wise, we begin to see it as the means by which dross is leached away so that we begin to move toward purity of heart. We are being weaned from the visible and impermanent world and trained to direct our gaze toward heaven. In such a situation, if we avail ourselves of the means at our disposal, we can put ourselves in the way of receiving comfort from God, who says, "I am with you. Do not be afraid." Despite appearance and our strong sense of abandonment, we are not alone. If we live long and keep faith we will probably experience for ourselves the truth of what Helder Camara wrote in his poem "Put Your Ear to the Ground": "The Lord is there. / He is far less likely / to abandon us / in hardship / than in times of ease." To some extent, suffering is a call to disinvest ourselves of concern for the present or reaction to it and, instead, to stretch out our desire toward the future of which faith is a foretaste. But we need to keep consolidating our confidence in God's goodwill toward us:

> Fear thou not, for I am with thee. Be not afraid, for I am your God. I will strengthen thee and help thee, and I will sustain thee with the right hand of my justice. Behold all that provoke thee shall be ashamed and confounded;

> they shall be as nothing, and they that strive with thee shall perish. Thou shall seek them and shalt not find them: to wit the men of thy strife, for they shall be as nothing and the men that war against thee as a thing of naught. For I the Lord your God will hold thy right hand, saying unto thee, "Fear not, I will help thee. Fear not, thou worm Jacob and ye men of Israel, I will help thee," saith the Lord and thy redeemer, the holy one of Israel. (Isa 41:10–14)

The Servant relies on God's sustaining support, not only in light momentary afflictions but also in more chronic trials, where he has to endure violence and ignominy and failure over a long period. If we look at the ancient narratives of martyrdom, it seems that these chosen ones went to their death full of joy and devoid of any resentment. It is as though the worse the exterior trouble became, the more intense the interior experience of divine comfort. There must have been some interior counterweight that made it possible for the saints to endure severe hardships without cracking. It could only have been that, through many years, they had developed deep habits of prayer that enabled them to draw strength from God, not only to endure difficult times but, in some mysterious way, to thrive because of them.

Service is made concrete in the fulfillment of the mission assigned. It is by engaging in the tasks that have been committed that the Servant finds his own identity and experiences all the nuances of his relationship with God. Both positive and negative experiences have something to contribute. It is important that servanthood is more an interior disposition than merely the accomplishment of particular exterior obligations. True service is generous and joyful. Somehow or other, it must plot a middle course between voluntary service, on the one hand, and servitude and servility, on the other. It is offered freely but in a spirit of detachment from visible rewards.

Georges Auzou titled his study of the Book of Exodus *From Servitude to Service*. This is the journey we all have to make on the way to experiencing the freedom of God's children. Finally, we begin to do naturally and joyfully what initially was done fearfully and under constraint. We will be lucky if we can complete the transition within the forty years that Israel spent in the wilderness. The spirit of servanthood is something that develops slowly. Auzou describes it thus:

> "Service" has become an ensemble of dispositions of the heart and of the spirit, of the whole person. An attitude and a life animated by a deep faith, a religious outlook which impregnates the whole of existence in the gift of self, devotion, attentive obedience, and perfect fidelity. This service is a function of love—the generous search for the Lord who is loved and a zeal to keep his commandments. Here it is that the words and realities of the Old Testament find their fulfilment in the New Testament. Jesus will be the Servant of God *par excellence*. And in Christ Jesus, his disciple Christians, can also, if they wish, serve God in truth.[5]

The attitude of service is something very beautiful. It derives from a lifetime spent in conscious dependence on God. It is powerfully and placidly evoked by Psalm 123. Despite deep disgrace, the faithful servant remains attentive, waiting for deliverance from God:

> To you who dwell in the heavens
> have I lifted up my eyes.

[5] Georges Auzou, *De la servitude au service:* étude du livre de *l'Exode* (Paris: Éditions de l'Orante, 1961), 82.

As the eyes of a servant
are on the hands of his master,
as the eyes of a handmaid
are on the hands of her mistress,
so are our eyes on the Lord our God,
waiting for mercy.

Have mercy, O Lord, have mercy
for we are full of much contempt.
Our very soul is full of much contempt,
scorned by the rich,
despised by the proud.

4

Glory

We have already reflected on the transcendent otherness of God. The being of God is so dense that it cannot be contained within the limits of the created world nor comprehended by the sharpest efforts of the created mind. The being of God is untouched by anything that eventuates in the world of space and time. Influence is unidirectional. God is Lord of history because, by the ongoing act of creation, God is a determining force on whatever happens on earth. The act itself, however, comes entirely from God's own initiative and is not prompted by anything outside itself. This unconditioned otherness is the divine mode of being; our minds can begin to grasp what it means only through the various channels by which the selfhood of God has been manifested to us. What God *is* must be considered as beyond our direct knowing, but we can see for ourselves what God *does*.

In the Hebrew Bible, the word for "glory" is *kabod*.[1] The word-family to which this term belongs has connotations of heaviness, substance, wealth, or power. Its opposites include notions of lightness or insubstantiality. The glory of God was considered to express a certain radiance or splendor. It was the visible impact of God's intervention in human affairs. We see this

[1] The English word "glory" occurs 437 times in the New Revised Standard Version of the Bible.

in the events associated with Israel's exodus from Egypt (see Exod 29:43). God's presence is conceived as a preternatural fire:

> Then Moses went up to the mount, and the cloud covered the mountain. And the glory of the Lord abode upon mount Sinai, and the cloud covered it six days: and the seventh day he called unto Moses out of the midst of the cloud. And the sight of the glory of the Lord was like consuming fire on the top of the mountain, in the eyes of the children of Israel. And Moses entered into the midst of the cloud, and went up to the mountain: and Moses was in the mount forty days and forty nights. (Exod 24:15–18)

Making contact with the divine reality introduces the human being into a sphere in which the senses are overwhelmed and the intellectual faculties clouded. Not from want of meaning but because of its abundance. Saint Paul will say "superabundance." Yet with the attraction to enter the vortex is a hint of a threat. God's glory is a consuming fire. No one can see God and live. We can approach God only by means of the channels, which God has established. We dare not presume to come close to God through our own devising.

The reality of God is self-diffusive, that is to say, it belongs to the divine nature to bring forth into being that which is not. The divine radiance is an expression of this extroverting energy of God. This is a theological proposition that is difficult for us to comprehend, since God is complete and self-sufficient and has no need of any external reality. The catechism answer to the question, "Why did God make the world?" brings little enlightenment. "St. Bonaventure explains that God created all things 'not to increase his glory, but to show it forth and communicate it.'"[2] We find ourselves compelled to leave speculation on the divine motivation

---

2 *Catechism of the Catholic Church*, §293.

for the entertainment of theologians and, instead, to concentrate simply on the fact that God has chosen to engage in self-revelation to the human family. The outshining of divine glory is expressed in God's self-revelation.

The sapiential literature of the Old Testament often celebrates the truth that God's first act of self-manifestation was creation. "The skies proclaim the glory of God" (Ps 19:1). Unlike some of the myths of Mesopotamia, the created world was not the detritus of a cataclysmic battle between deities. It emerged as a result of a word effortlessly spoken by God. And, with each word, creation becomes richer and more differentiated until the wondrous emergence of a creature, sufficiently intelligent to be considered the image and likeness of God. In all creation, nothing is so like God as the human being. The image is imperfect, precarious, and transient, but at its best, it is more highly suggestive of what God is like than any other visible creature. The human being is a real though faint expression of the outpouring of God's glory. Nothing else in our created world is closer to God.

In his opening verses, Second Isaiah sets forth the promise that is the core of his proclamation. "And the glory of the Lord will be revealed, and all flesh will see it together" (40:5). But this is a promise that is always in a state of realization. Divine self-manifestation is not only the future, it is the permanent condition of the relation between the Creator and what has been created. We can readily perceive the effects of this outreach in the world around us, but more often than not, we fail to follow the trail that leads us to make contact with the source from which all visible creation depends. The future will be glorious only when all sentient beings acknowledge the God who is the first and last (44:6) and who will not yield place to any other (42:8). This is the mission of God's servants: to facilitate the reinsertion of creatures into the circle of life that connects them with the divine. All alike come from God; their present existence will be harmonious and joyful to the extent that they give themselves to returning to their point of origin.

How can we know what direction to take when we are surrounded by so many incompatible alternatives? God is hidden from us (45:15). How can we begin to reorient our lives when we cannot locate the end of the journey? This is a barrier we are unable to breach on our own. A solution is possible only because God takes the initiative. God's outgoing energy becomes tangible in human history by spoken words. The self-revelation of God is achieved not only in creation and in mighty acts of power; it submits itself to the constriction of human language. The energy of God is so powerful that when it activates the human spirit, it enables one to follow the tracks of God's actions back to their source. We begin to perceive something of that reality on which we are dependent for our being and to observe it at work in the world around us, especially in acts of salvation. God's saving activity can, thus, be perpetuated by words that convey the good news to later generations—words that not only inform but also communicate energy.

In Israel's history, the saving acts of God were not only experienced; they were also understood to be acts of God. A record of them was handed on from generation to generation. Parents passed on the good news to their children. Institutions were created that preserved the memory. In this way, the past was continually being made present, and people of today's generation were able to participate in events that happened long ago. This traditional memory was eventually cast into writing that served as a criterion to guide the corporate remembering. This record is what we know as the Bible. For the Jewish people, it was especially the five books of the Pentateuch, which were held to be normative of all religious practice. This was *torah* or "teaching" par excellence, although the term itself could also be applied more broadly.

The glory of God is manifested by *torah*. Not only a teaching that is contained in books, but a teaching that is preserved in memory, in the heart. A teaching that is made visible by external practice and by a manner of living. *Torah* is made concrete in *mishpat* that is through a way of life or a rule of law that is conditioned by God's self-revelation. Living in accordance with *torah* leads to righteousness, *sedaqah*, at a community level and for individuals. *Torah*, *mishpat*, and *sedaqah*, each in its own way, are manifestations of the glory of God. In some subtle way, they demonstrate to us what God is.

Let us examine each of these concepts in a little more detail.

TORAH

In the first place, we are offered God's gift of *torah*. This word is usually translated "law," a term that unnecessarily restricts our understanding of the full scope of its meaning, since its fundamental meaning is more general.[3] It derives from the verb *yarah*, which means "throw" and, thence, to point out, direct, teach, or instruct. The noun, *torah*, is much better rendered by a more open word such as "teaching." A necessary part of the divine guidance is instruction concerning appropriate human behavior; laws are only a part of that guidance. The divine influence is broader than material lawmaking about what to do and what to omit doing. The advent of God requires of us a whole new vision of what life is about. The reception of that revelation inevitably requires a recalibration of one's value system. After an encounter with the All-Holy, nothing remains the same.

---

[3] The Septuagint translation of the Hebrew Scriptures into Greek from about the third century before Christ translated the word by *nomos*, which does mean "law." This coincided with the rise of the petty legalism associated with rabbinic Judaism, with its counting of 613 commandments—obviously, not of equal importance but, as the Epistle of James points out, to fail in a single observance is to be guilty of abandoning the whole Law. This tendency, in turn, may have been accentuated by the break in tradition brought about by the Babylonian exile. As a result, revelation came to be identified with its practical demands, and God came to be seen both as lawgiver and judge. The Latin use of the harsh-sounding monosyllable *lex* added to the process of hardening.

Most of us approach the understanding of the term *torah* influenced by a simplistic understanding of Saint Paul's polarizing distinction of grace and law. "You are not under the Law but under grace" (Rom 6:14). In some sense, we see *torah* as the enemy of faith and grace. In this context, "gospel" and "law" are diametric opposites. Especially since the time of Immanuel Kant, we view all heteronomy as something to be minimized. Without referring to concrete legislative measures, what we mean by "law" has become abstract and universalized as something that inhibits our freedom. We need to be on our guard that our appreciation of *torah* is not diminished by our reservations about the role of "law" in our life.

The many words that strive to express what is being revealed by God can be no more than approximations. The divine reality can never be fully encompassed by human language. Words are not only limited in themselves, they are also restricted by the capacities of those who hear them. If I were to teach quantum physics to kindergarten children, my exposition would scarcely do justice to the topic, not because of any inadequacy in the teacher (of course), but because I must address myself to the limited receptivity of the students. When God self-reveals, even the best of us are unable to receive the whole message, not only because our spiritual intelligence is limited, but also because language itself is incapable of communicating something that is beyond its capacity to comprehend.

The heart of Old Testament religion was communicated when God spoke to Moses face-to-face; his efforts to transcribe the practical consequences of this revelation on tablets of stone were entirely secondary and infinitely inferior to what he had experienced atop the mountain. The word of God allows itself to be shaped by the situation of the receiver. This is the "abbreviated word which God sends upon the earth" (Rom 9:28 and Isa 10:22 [Vulgate]). It accommodates itself to our limitations. Even so, the impact on us is manifold. When God's glory is revealed by the word, as Psalm 19 reminds us, it revives the soul, gives wisdom to the simple, gladdens the heart, and gives light to the eyes. And much more. No single term can encompass the impact that God's word has on the human heart: it is a call, an invitation, an assurance, a message of love and acceptance, a word of guidance, an instruction, a prescription, an admonishment, a correction, a judgment, and a rebuke. We find all these messages throughout the Bible, including Second Isaiah. God's word, God's *torah*, however, cannot be limited to one of these; it is all of them, simultaneously. We, however, perceive only a single aspect at a time.

It is God's self-revelation that is the beginning of real religion. This is something that lifts humankind beyond its limited vision of right and wrong based on natural law and social expectations. The revelation of God relativizes every human norm and rule. Nothing can be the same again. But, as is clear from the psalms, this revelation is not a burden but a source of joy and happiness. "Blessed are those who walk in the *torah* of the Lord." It is good news. It is the beginning of a pathway to a more abundant life. The commandments are like safety rails along the roadside. They are meant to prevent us from hurling ourselves headlong off the track into the dangerous thickets that surround it. Commandments are secondary. Revelation is what matters most.

Torah must be considered as the outshining of the divine glory, the sum total of God's manifold acts of self-revelation, and much more. So overwhelming is its density that its impact on us is both fearsome and fascinating—to use the terms employed in Rudolf Otto's *The Idea of the Holy*.[4] Yet the transcendent otherness of God prompts us to a certain wariness. We are out of our depth and so we must take care not to endanger ourselves by an uninvited familiarity. Remember the terrifying story of Uzzah, son of Abinadab. In a well-meaning gesture meant to prevent

---

[4] Rudolf Otto, *The Idea of the Holy*, trans. W. Harvey (London: Oxford University Press, 1980).

the Ark of the Covenant from toppling over, Uzzah reached out to steady it, "but the Lord was angry and struck him down for his imprudent action and he died there beside the Ark of God" (2 Sam 6:6–7). Like the Ark of the Covenant, *torah* demands ultimate respect, expressed practically by compliance with its demands. But, simultaneously, *torah* binds us to itself by infinite attractiveness, animating and energizing us at every level of our being. When we are touched by the divine glory, we become more fully alive, more fully human. And we want more.

"The glory of God is the living human, and the vision of God is the life of the human."[5] The purpose of the outshining of God's glory is to lead human beings to the vision of God, and, thereby, to the joyous fulfillment of the inherent potentialities of their nature. The word of God accomplishes this by contrasting strategies. It can be stern—laying down commandments that limit our options and seek to confine our behavior within prescribed limits. Revelation can also be alluring—kindling within us a desire for what is beyond our earthly experience, a yearning for infinity. These are, as it were, the two feet that propel our progress toward the vision of God, restraining our instinctual impulses and, simultaneously, giving full scope to our yearning for what is beyond us.

For Second Isaiah, the universal manifestation of divine glory means, in practical terms, that all will be instructed by *torah* in the ways that lead to the vision of God and hence to life. As envisaged by Jeremiah this will be realized when "no one will need to teach others saying, 'know the Lord.' All will know me from the least to the greatest, says the Lord" (Jer 31:34). All alike will have been caught up in a cosmic return to its Origin.

From the postexilic period onward, *torah* began to replace Temple as the center of Jewish religion. It became the primary object of the religious feeling among the Jewish diaspora—one

---

[5] Saint Irenaeus, *Adversus Haereses* IV.20.7; *Sources Chrétiennes* 100, pp. 648–49.

less likely to be demolished by external enemies. If we consider *torah* only in terms of obligation and dread, we will be divorced from its enlivening and celebratory aspects and easily fall prey to discouragement. In Judaism, the conclusion of the annual cycle of readings of *Torah* is celebrated by a feast of rejoicing. It is a joyous holiday that celebrates the Jewish love of *torah* and study. *Simchat Torah* (Rejoicing in the Law) is celebrated by taking all the *Torah* scrolls out of the ark in the synagogue and spending the evening dancing, singing, and rejoicing.[6] The scrolls are carried around the sanctuary in seven circles called *hakafot*. Each circle is accompanied by a prayer for deliverance, followed by verses from Psalm 119. The pleas for deliverance are addressed to the Lord, as the speaker of righteousness, as the pure and upright One, as the knower of thoughts, as the king of the worlds, as the helper of the needy, and as the holy and awesome One. The *Shacharit* prayer that follows the reading of *Torah* begins,

> Rejoice and exult on *Simchat Torah* and pay homage to the *Torah*, for its goods are superior to all other goods, more precious than fine gold and gems. Let us delight and rejoice with this Torah, for it is our life, our strength and our light.[7]

MISHPAT

From *torah* flows *mishpat*. The first Servant Song begins, "Behold my servant whom I uphold, my chosen one in whom my soul delights. I will impart my Spirit to him so that he will bring forth *mishpat* for the nations" (Isa 42:1). The term is frequently translated "justice" or "judgment," but many other suggested

---

[6] Simchat Torah is a Jewish holiday that celebrates and marks the conclusion of the annual cycle of public Torah readings, and the beginning of a new cycle.

[7] *Tehillat Hashem* (Brooklyn, NY: Merkos L'Inyonei Chinuch, 1982), 336–38.

renderings have been offered. No single suggestion is completely satisfactory because "*mishpat* repeatedly transcends the boundaries of the various specialized meanings."[8]

The basic context of the term is its connection to the verb *shapat*, which moves around on a continuum from "rule" to "judge," thus touching both executive and judicial authority. The "judges" in the biblical book of that name were mostly rulers, according to our way of thinking. From the notion of judging flows meanings such as "giving judgment," "doing justice," and "establishing justice." When applied to God, the verb usually means bringing about justice, bringing his adversary to court (Isa 43:26), discerning between the good and the wicked, giving the nations justice (51:5), and punishing evildoers.

It is often hard to find exact English equivalents to Hebrew terms that evolved over a number of centuries. I would suggest that one contemporary meaning of *mishpat* would be something like "the rule of law" and, thence, "the state of one who lives by the rule of law." Even when it seems to describe a subjective disposition, it retains a forensic element since such a state involves objective conformity with certain standards of behavior. It is understood that these moral norms have been inspired by *torah*. Thus, this word refers to those whose lives are governed by their reception of God's self-revelation. In some cases, such as Psalm 119, the terms *torah* and *mishpat* seem so closely linked as to be almost synonymous:

> Who hath measured the waters in his fist, and counted heaven with his span, and comprehended the dust of the earth in a measure, and weighed the mountains in a weight and the hills in a balance? Who hath instructed the Spirit of the Lord or was his counselor or taught him? Of whom took he counsel and who instructed him in

---

[8] Bo Johnson, s.v. "*mishpat*," in *Theological Dictionary of the Old Testament* (Grand Rapids, MI: Eerdmans, 2003), 9:95.

> the way of judgment (*mishpat*) or taught him knowledge, and showed unto him the way of understanding. Behold the nations are as a drop of a bucket, and are counted as the dust of the balance. (Isa 40:12–15)

Mishpat takes its origin from God for whom there is no need for instruction in its ways. *Mishpat* is the cosmic harmony given by the Creator. It transcends morality. The order envisaged by God is not merely a matter of people behaving appropriately; it involves a return to the primal harmony of Paradise. Its extent is beyond what humans can formulate or nations strive to implement. It is the divine order, as yet inexperienced, but capable of fulfillment to the extent that the way of *torah* is followed. *Mishpat* and *torah* belong together. "'Judgment' and 'law' together convey the idea of revelation, the revelation which in Israel's history is initiated in the patriarchal period and takes form in the covenant of Sinai."[9] Establishing *mishpat* involves bringing human society into harmony with the multifaceted self-revelation of God.

The Lord's servant is given the task to bring *mishpat* not only to Israel but to the nations (41:1) and further, through his own fidelity to his mission (41:3), also to the whole earth (41:4). Second Isaiah envisages a future in which the whole of humanity lives by God's self-revelation; the order given to creation at its beginning is to be restored for the fulfillment of humankind and the glory of God. The Servant is engaged in a task totally beyond his own competence to fulfill. It is not his work alone, it is primarily God's work since, through it, the divine glory will attain its intended completeness.

The establishment of God's rule on earth means that temporal kingdoms will enjoy only a relative permanence—they are no more than a drop in a bucket. The reign of God necessarily involves the suppression of every claim to absolute authority.

---

[9] John L. McKenzie, *Second Isaiah* (New York: Doubleday, 1968), 37.

It will be experienced by earthly rulers as a revolutionary insurgence, and every effort will be made to resist it. Those who have been given the mission of actively promoting God's reign will inevitably face persecution and rejection. This was certainly the lot of the prophet Jeremiah. "And they said, 'Come, let us make a plan against Jeremiah. The *torah* will not be lost to the priest, nor counsel from the sage nor the word from the prophet'" (Jer 18:18). The ultimate gift of divine self-revelation is known by the undeviating resistance it generates.

Mishpat is further explained by its association with other terms such as *sedaqah*, usually translated as "righteousness" or an equivalent.[10] In Psalm 99, a clear linkage is made between three related concepts: "The King is mighty and loves *mishpat*. You have established equity [*mesharim*], and brought about *mishpat*, and *sedaqah* in Jacob" (Ps 99:3). And in Psalm 33 "[The Lord] loves *sedaqah* and *mishpat*; the earth is full of the Lord's mercy [*chesed*]" (Ps 33:5). The meanings are interrelated and overlapping, with no clear boundaries between them.

SEDAQAH

Linked with *mishpat* is *sedaqah*. This family of words occurs 523 times in the Old Testament: the nouns *sedaqah* 157 times and *sedeq* 119 times, the verb *sadeq* 41 times, and the adjective *saddiq* 206 times.[11] As with any term used over hundreds of years and in

---

[10] Older Catholic translations preferred "justice" as the normal rendering, following the Vulgate *iustitia*. For some, the term "righteous" had negative connotations of "self-righteous." A problem that arises with translating *sedaqah* as *iustitia* or "justice" is that it becomes identified with one of the four cardinal virtues of Classical Greek philosophy. More recently it is sometimes further reduced to imply social justice; it is wider than that.

[11] As noted by Bo Johnson in the *Theological Dictionary of the Old Testament*, (Grand Rapids, MI: Eerdmans, 2003), 12:239–69. "Although *sedeq* and *sedaqa* are in many instances interchangeable, they cannot really be treated as synonyms; *sedeq* evokes the notion of correctness and order,

different contexts, it is useless to seek a single equivalent in another language. It can signify righteous activity, the disposition from which this derives, or its effect in shaping and administering a just social order. Probably this virtuous activity is more often seen as horizontal rather than vertical, and as expressed in concrete actions rather than as an abstract inner quality. It can be attributed to God as well as to human beings, in which case it often refers to God's saving activity and its effects in bringing about harmony and well-being on earth. Thus, it is linked with words evoking the divine mercy and compassion.

By my count, the family of words appears 29 times in Second Isaiah, and is variously translated.[12] More than a third of these instances refer to the divine righteousness, the source from which all human righteousness derives. As in the rest of the Bible, the meaning of these terms reaches out and touches many qualities that may be considered positive: faithfulness, innocence, mercy,

---

while *sedaqa* emphasizes action and activity rather than condition. In this sense *sedaqa* represents *sedeq* functionally" (7:256). A competent and accessible summary of the range of meanings associated with these words in the Old Testament can be found in John L. McKenzie, "Righteous, Righteousness," in *Dictionary of the Bible* (London: Geoffrey Chapman, 1968), 739–41.

[12] Cf. Isa 41:2, 41:10, 41:26, 42:6, 42:21, 43:9, 43:26, 45:8 (bis), 45:13, 45:19, 45:21, 45:23, 45:24, 45:25, 46:12, 46:13, 48:1, 48:18 (the text of 49:24 is usually emended), 50:8, 51:1, 51:5, 51:6, 51:7, 51:8, 53:11 (bis), 54:13, 54:17. The New International Version renders these words as: righteousness (20), right (4), vindication (2), innocence (1), integrity (1), and justification (1). The New Revised Standard Version as: righteousness (12), right (4), deliverance (4), victory or triumph (3), vindication (2), justification or making righteous (2), success (1), prosperity (1). The Jerusalem Bible as: integrity (8), victory (7), right (3), deliverance (1), directness (1), innocence (1), justification (1), justice (1), salvation (1), triumph (1), and vindication (1); one occurrence (53:11) is left untranslated. The Revised English Bible as: victory (11), righteousness (4), right (3), deliverance (2), justice (2), clear his name (1), justification (1), sincerity (1), success (1), triumph (1), truth (1); one occurrence (53:11) is left untranslated. The Geneva Bible, which we are using, as: righteousness (18), justice (6), and justification (5).

uprightness, truthfulness, justice. Such qualities may be considered to be the result of living in accordance with the covenant between God and Israel. Keeping to the terms of the covenant had a transformative effect—not only through the large-heartedness of *chesed*, but also through the well-ordered relationships of *sedaqah*, which set a solid foundation for a cohesive community that lives in accordance with God's *torah*. "God manifests his own beneficent righteousness by giving human beings his law, and corresponding human righteousness consists in living in accordance with that law."[13]

It is through the covenant that God's *sedaqah* is revealed. The glory of God is the manifestation of God's active righteousness, which has the effect of rendering righteous everything that it touches. Its effect is salvation: "I am bringing my righteousness near: it is not far distant. Nor will my salvation be delayed" (Isa 46:13). There is a kind of reciprocity in righteousness. By God's action, it descends from above and, as a result, also rises from below. "You heavens, rain down *sedeq* from above and clouds pour it forth; let the earth open and salvation spring up and with it *sedeqah*; I, the Lord, have created it" (45:8). The outpouring of divine righteousness causes salvation and righteousness to flourish on the earth. The initiative is God's, who begins the process with no antecedent prompting. The communication of righteousness continues the work of creation. "They will say of me, 'In the Lord alone are *sedaqah* and strength.' . . . In the Lord all the seed of Israel will be made righteous and will rejoice" (45:24–25). God is the sole source of righteousness. Any who are righteous are so because God has made them so. And the effect of God's overflowing righteousness is a blessing for those who allow themselves to be shaped by it. "If only you had paid attention to my commandments, then your peace would have been like a

---

[13] Bo Johnson, s.v. "*sadaq*," *Theological Dictionary of the Old Testament*, 12:261.

river, and your righteousness like waves in the ocean" (48:18). Meanwhile because of hardheartedness, righteousness is lacking (46:12); it must be actively sought (51:5).

* * *

The outshining of God's glory is overwhelmingly practical. It brings salvation to humanity by showing us the path to a more abundant life—provided that we are willing to be humbly receptive of that guidance. "The glory of God is lacking to human beings; in no way can they receive it except by service directed to God."[14] God's glory is a summons to humanity to live godlier lives. Mysteriously, inherent in the call there is energy to do what otherwise would be impossible. The divine light not only reveals; it also empowers.

Glory belongs uniquely to God. It is an otherness that nothing in the world of space and time can claim or mimic: "I will not give my glory to another" (42:8, 48:11); "I am the first and the last; apart from me there is no god" (44:6). Idols are an abomination precisely because they have no power to give evidence of the qualities attributed to them by their followers (40:19–20, 41:21–24, 42:17, 44:9–20). Although God's inner being is hidden (cf. 45:15), God's glory has been revealed (cf. 40:5) in creation and covenant and in the gift of *torah*. To receive glory is to become a hearer of the Word and thus to enter into a relationship with God, without which human life is a tragedy. Such a crippling loss recalls the biblical story of the son of Phineas who was named Ichabod because "Glory has departed from Israel" (1 Sam 4:21–22). To the extent that glory departs from life, chaos returns. There will be a famine of hearing God's word (cf. Amos 8:11).

The glory of God is revealed to us to be our guide and protection through the vicissitudes of life: "the Lord will go before you; the God of Israel will be the guard behind you" (Isa 52:12). Our journey through life will be like the Israelites'

---

[14] Saint Irenaeus, *Adversus Haereses* IV.16.4; SChr 100, pp. 568–70.

forty-year trek through the wilderness. We will not escape difficulties, struggles, and defeats, but God will accompany us through fire and through water:

> When thou passest through the waters I will be with thee, and through the floods that they do not overflow thee. When thou walkest through the very fire, thou shalt not be burnt, neither shall the flame kindle upon thee. For I am the Lord your God, the holy one of Israel, thy Saviour. (Isa 43:2–3)

> Thus saith the Lord which maketh a way in the Sea, and a path in the mighty waters. When he bringeth out the chariot and horse, the army and the power lie together and shall not rise, they are extinct and quenched as [a wick]. (Isa 43:16–17)

Because God is with us there is no cause for us to be afraid. The sources of our troubles, which seem so powerful to us, will disappear. Those whom the outreach of God touches need have no fear of any lesser reality. "If God is for us, who is against us?" (Rom 8:31). God's protection is not only defensive; it is aggressively offensive:

> The Lord shall go forth as a giant, he shall stir up his courage like a man of war; he shall shout and cry and shall prevail against his enemies. (Isa 42:13)

> Fear thou not, for I am with thee, be not afraid for I am your God. I will strengthen thee and help thee, and will sustain thee with the right hand of my justice. Behold all that provoke thee shall be ashamed and confounded; they shall be as nothing, and they that strive with thee shall perish. Thou shall seek them and shalt not find them, to wit, the men of thy strife, for they shall be as nothing, and

> the men that war against thee, as a thing of naught. For I the Lord your God will hold thy right hand, saying unto thee, Fear not, I will help thee. (Isa 41:10–12)

Marching forth under the shadow of the Most High, our long journey through the seemingly hostile wilderness becomes a triumphant progress. With each forward step, we come close to the dawning of a new age in which God's glory will be untrammeled and the whole world will be awash with uninhibited joy:

> Rejoice ye heavens for the Lord hath done it. Shout ye lower parts of the earth, brast forth into praises ye mountains, O forest and every tree therein; for the Lord hath redeemed Jacob and will be glorified in Israel. (Isa 44:23)

> Rejoice O heavens and be joyful O earth, brast forth into praise O mountains. For God hath comforted his people and will have mercy on his afflicted. (Isa 49:13)

> O ye desolate places of Jerusalem, be glad and rejoice together: for the Lord hath comforted his people: he hath redeemed Jerusalem. (Isa 52:9)

This is the note on which Second Isaiah concludes: a faith in God's power of deliverance that is so strong that its exuberant happiness cannot be contained, but communicates itself to the whole of creation.

> Rejoice, O barren that didst not bear: break forth into joy and rejoice thou that did not travail with child: for the desolate hath more children than the married wife, saith the Lord. (Isa 54:1)

> Therefore, ye shall go out with joy and be led forth with peace: the mountains and the hills shall break forth

> before you into joy, and all the trees of the field shall clap their hands. For thorns there shall grow fig trees: for nettles shall grow the myrrh tree, and it shall be to the Lord for a name and for an everlasting sign that shall not be taken away. (Isa 55:12–13)

The reception of God's glory inclines the receiver to give back the glory to God. This is done not only by spontaneous acts of admiring praise, but also by the more formal medium of psalmody, in which God is reverently blessed.

> Sing unto the Lord a new song and his praise from the end of the earth, ye that go down to the sea and all that is therein, the isles and inhabitants thereof. Let the wilderness and the cities thereof lift up their voice, the towns that Kedar doth inhabit. Let the inhabitants of the rocks sing, let them shout from the top of the mountains. Let them give glory unto the Lord and declare his praise in the islands. (Isa 42:10–12)

The glory of God is God's self-revelation communicated to us through human agency and becoming part of our universal human patrimony. By initiating a dialogue with us, God calls us to enter within the glory and to discover for ourselves that God's self-revelation is living and active, well able to accomplish in our midst all that God purposed from the very beginning of the creation process. In the end, God will be all in all, and there will be a new heaven and a new earth. "Salvation is near for those who fear God, so that glory will dwell in our land" (Ps 85:10).

5

SIN

In reading the Book of Genesis, we are immediately confronted with the reality of sin in the primal disobedience of Adam and Eve. As we read on, we perceive the burgeoning of human resistance and rebellion in parallel with the many merciful interventions of God. As we continue our way through the narrative books of the Old Testament, starting from the front of the Bible, we pick up the message that sin is like some form of contagion that multiplies exponentially with the passage of time. And while we may understand that sin consists in a state of alienation from God expressed through disobedience and rebellion, the nature of sin remains unclear. Saint Paul speaks about a *mysterium iniquitatis,* the mystery of lawlessness (2 Thess 2:7), a theme that has long occupied the attention of philosophers. Bernard Lonergan categorizes the failure of free will to choose a morally obligatory course of action or reject its opposite as a "surd." It lacks all intelligibility.[1] It has no meaning because it is the negation

[1] Bernard Lonergan, *Insight: A Study of Human Understanding* (London: Longmans, Green and Co., 1957), 666–67. A fuller descriptive definition of foundational sin includes such terms as: meaninglessness, emptiness, futility, insignificance, purposelessness, vanity, worthlessness, hollowness, pointlessness, uselessness, senselessness, ineffectiveness, idleness, fruitlessness, vainness, bootlessness, ineffectuality, frivolousness, unprofitableness, unavailingness, aimlessness, hopelessness, barrenness, valuelessness, insin-

of reason. As such, it becomes visible only in its effects that are in wrongful actions. These are symptoms, and not the disease itself. Sins (plural) can be seen and assessed; their ultimate source, sin (singular), remains a mystery not to be explained away by excuses or extenuating circumstances. It is beyond psychology or sociology. The story of Adam and Eve and their reason-defying act of disobedience is an attempt to dramatize this recalcitrant negativity to which we are all prone. This is the original sin. This underlying and all-pervasive sin preexists any active choice on our part; its power can be experienced only in the effort and the act of resisting it and neutralizing it.

The collective state resulting from such a condition was termed by many medieval authors *miseria*. This was more than the subjective misery that many of us experience. It was seen as the universal condition of unredeemed humanity that was the basic cause of all negativity and of all particular wrongful acts, each of which strengthens the hold that sin has upon us. To be saved from this state requires an intervention from outside. As these authors used to say, *miseria* calls out for *misericordia*. Our "fallen" state cries out for mercy, for salvation. Salvation is not something that we ourselves can achieve; it is something gratuitously given by another.

The state of sinfulness is evoked in the Bible through a series of graphic images. Each in its own way underlines how, because of sin, we fall short of full humanity. Because of sin, our lives are defective and our joie de vivre is radically reduced. Every expression of sin is colored, in varying degrees, by all of the following metaphors.

---

cerity, inanity, unprofitability, triviality, abortiveness, unproductiveness, unimportance, sterility, unconvincingness, falseness, needlessness, stupidity, incompetence, inefficiency, unsuccessfulness, ineptness, insubstantiality, silliness, unreality, cheapness, absurdness, aridity, failure, forlornness, impotence. (Near-synonyms taken from a thesaurus.)

Illness: "Heal Me and I Shall Be Healed" (Jer 17:14)

The possibility of a full humanity is reduced by illness, which disables and incapacitates us so that, when it invades our life, we are not willing or not able to do the things that are usually possible. In addition, some illnesses, such as leprosy, were considered to be the result of personal moral failure, and thus the sufferer had to endure the added burdens of social shame, rejection, and isolation. Not only the Pharisees, but also Jesus's own disciples, thought that for a man to be born blind, someone must have sinned (cf. John 9:2). Conversely, illness could serve as a metaphor for sin itself, so that the sinner could turn to God and ask for healing—not from sickness but from sin. Thus the Psalmist laments, "Through my sin, there is no health in my limbs" (38:3); "Lord, do not reprove me in your anger; punish me not, in your rage. Have mercy on me, Lord, I have no strength; my soul is racked with pain" (6:2); and "As for me, I said: Lord, have mercy on me, heal my soul for I have sinned against you" (41:4). Healing comes only from God. "It is God who forgives all your guilt, who heals every one of your ills" (Ps 103:3). In this case, we are praying for liberation from the dire consequences of personal and social sin and not primarily for relief from bodily illness.

Uncleanness: "Wash Away My Iniquity and Cleanse Me from My Sin" (Ps 51:2)

Filth is not a terminal condition but something that reduces the attractiveness of a life and makes it repulsive. Sometimes it occurs as the result of illness and has the effect of increasing its ignominy. The prophet Ezekiel, especially, often speaks about "defilement," which adds a moral nuance to the notion. Uncleanness is a powerful image of alienation from God in many spiritual traditions. In an effort to reduce its impact, ritual washings are prescribed. These are considered as symbolic.

Usually, it is less a matter of washing off physical dirt as of enacting a ritual by which the unseen desolation wrought by sin can be restored to wholeness. The priestly tradition, and later the Pharisees, made much of such ritual washings. These rituals also inspired metaphorical usage for God's saving intervention: "Oh, sprinkle me by hyssop and I shall be made clean: wash me and I shall become whiter than snow" (Ps 51:7). The opposite of uncleanness is purity. Jesus, however, put the emphasis less on bodily cleanliness than on inner purity of heart: "It is not what goes into persons from outside that can make them unclean, but it is what comes out of persons that makes them unclean" (Mark 7:15).

LOSTNESS: "I AM LOST LIKE A SHEEP; SEEK YOUR SERVANT" (PS 119:176)

Sin unseats the rational basis of our lives in favor of temporary or delusional advantage. Our absorption in the present moment causes us to lose our bearings, and our ultimate destination fades from our view. In colonial Australian art, the "Lost Child" was an important trope, expressing a widespread anxiety about the prospect of being abandoned in an alien landscape. Being lost is more than a geographical malfunction. It is a state of terror at being unable to be certain about the immediate future. The next step is unclear because we cannot ascertain where we go after that. We are both fearful and paralyzed. If we do attempt to move, it is likely that we will end up walking in circles—an outward sign of our inner confusion. "The wicked walk around in circles" (Ps 12:9). Turning away from God causes us to lose the sense of where we are and where we should be going. "And God looked on the earth and, behold, it was corrupt, for all flesh had caused its way on the earth to become corrupt" (Gen 6:12). Because of their evil lives, the way no longer opened out before them. "The way of the wicked leads nowhere" (Ps 1:5). They have become like stupid sheep that have strayed from the flock and are unable to find a way of return.[2] "We all like sheep have gone astray, each of us turned to our own way" (Isa 53:6). Unless we are sought out by another, we will be irretrievably and permanently lost. The sense of being lost can also apply to being swamped by delusion, lost in a miasma of untruth, as Psalm 36 proclaims: "Sin whispers to the sinner in the depth of his heart. . . . He so flatters himself in his mind that he knows not his guilt" (Ps 36:1–2). And this even before the Golden Age of fake news!

DARKNESS: "GIVE LIGHT TO MY EYES LEST I FALL ASLEEP IN DEATH" (PS 13:3)

We are lost because we do not know where we are and we cannot see the way ahead. It is as though we are enveloped in a thick darkness. Like the land of Egypt that for three days was covered in a darkness so dense it could be felt (Exod 10:21), sin has the effect of blinding those whom it controls so that not only do they not perceive the malice of their wrongful deeds, but they may even consider those deeds praiseworthy.[3] The darkness of sin calls to mind the condition of chaos before the creation of light: an aggressive state of meaningless confusion. In the New Testament, the remediation of sin is often compared to enlightenment, the dawning of a new day, the replacement of darkness with light. Sin makes us both blind and deaf; it isolates us in our self-sufficiency so that we are left without the comfort and support of others.

---

[2] See also Jer 50:6, Zech 11:16, Matt 10:6, 15:24, 18:12–14, Luke 15:3–7, 1 Pet 2:25.

[3] Thus, Bernard of Clairvaux: "This stage is to be reckoned not as a mere fall but as the annihilation which belongs to final damnation, when the sinner has the harlot's face, unable to blush but only to scorn, incapable of distinguishing what is right from one's own wishes" (*Sententiae* 3.98; *Sancti Bernardi Opera* 6b.162. See also *The Steps of Humility and Pride* 51; *Sancti Bernardi Opera* 3.54–55).

GUILT: "TO YOU ALL FLESH WILL COME WITH ITS BURDEN OF SIN" (PS 65:3)

Sin is a weight that bears down upon us so that we are unable to do what otherwise would have been possible. "Our sins and offences weigh heavily upon us" (Ezek 33:10). "My iniquities loom over my head: they are a weight too heavy to bear" (Ps 38:4). Cumulative sinfulness is a burden that inhibits our native liveliness and makes the lightest of good works seem ponderous. It makes life seem like running a marathon in a wet overcoat. In addition, because most of us are unwilling to reform our behavior, we tend to push any sense of guilt beneath the level of consciousness. This increases the sense of being weighed down because denial inhibits our capacity to carry our load. Such repression may not be obvious to us, but it is evidenced by our tendency to imprint our own guilt onto others, looking on what they do with a jaundiced eye and unnecessarily condemning them for the very things of which we ourselves are guilty. Or guilt can manifest itself by obsessive actions that symbolically alleviate what we feel, such as washing our hands or cleaning our environment. Guilt consumes precious energy, and as a result we have less available for living. We cannot ourselves eliminate guilt—especially if it is well founded. We can, however, drown it by allowing ourselves to be flooded by the overwhelming experience of forgiveness and acceptance. "Even though our hearts condemn us, God is greater than our hearts and knows it all" (1 John 3:20). It is the awareness of the burden we carry that allows us to appreciate the generosity and gratuity of God's unconditional grace.

WARFARE: "HOW MANY ARE MY FOES, O LORD; HOW MANY ARE RISING AGAINST ME?" (PS 3:1)

"Is not human life on earth a time of military service?" (Job 7:1). Battle imagery is strong in the Old Testament and was later interpreted as a way of underlining the reality that avoiding wrongful actions is often a struggle, and one in which we fail more frequently than we would hope. The warfare is not always with external enemies. We find battles waging within ourselves between opposite tendencies. Notably, as Saint Paul describes, there is a constant tug-of-war between our noble aspirations to do good and the frequency with which we allow ourselves to be drawn into contrary modes of action. Sometimes people who attempt to pray the psalms find it difficult to identify with those passages that call down vengeance on enemies. These are best understood in the context of spiritual warfare: they are the subversive imaginations and habits of behavior that sabotage our best efforts to live lives of virtue, and it is right that we should inveigh against them. The ancients often attributed these hostile forces to demons; we would probably see them as coming from the dark side of our own nature. Our service of God can never be a time of indolence, and so, one of our most persistent temptations is a weariness born of discouragement. This is why the psalms often remind us that God is fighting on our side, as our avenger, or *go'el*. But God also operates in defensive mode. Psalm 18 begins, "I love you, O Lord my strength. The Lord is my rock, my fortress, my deliverer; my God my cliff where I take refuge. [God] is my shield and the horn of my rescue, my stronghold. I call to the Lord, who is worthy to be praised, and I am rescued from my enemies" (vv. 3–4). Those who recite the psalms often may well be surprised at how frequently God is referred to as a "shield."

ENSLAVEMENT: "HOW COULD WE SING THE LORD'S SONG IN A FOREIGN LAND?" (PS 137:4)

In the ancient world, warfare habitually led to the enslavement of those who had been on the losing side. Captives had to be ransomed or redeemed by payment to avoid being reduced to the half-life of slavery. The defeated nation was taken captive and reduced to servitude, as we see after the fall of Jerusalem, when nobles and a significant segment of the population were taken as prisoners to Babylon. Sin holds sinners captive, unable to free themselves from its grasp; someone else has to do it. "[God] will ransom Israel from all its evil" (Ps 130:8). Slavery continues as an image of sin in the New Testament. "[False prophets] promise them freedom, but they themselves are slaves to corruption, for people are enslaved to whatever controls them" (2 Pet 2:19). "Jesus answered them, 'Amen, amen, I say to you that everyone who commits sin is a slave of sin'" (John 8:34). The image is notably strong in the Epistle to the Romans:

> Do you not know that if you yield yourself to obey a master you are slaves of the master you obey, whether the master is sin leading to death, or obedience leading to righteousness? Once you were slaves of sin, but now, thank God, you have rendered sincere obedience to the form of teaching handed on to you. You have been freed from sin, you have become slaves of righteousness. . . . As you once yielded your members as slaves of impurity and lawlessness leading to lawlessness, so now yield them as slaves of righteousness leading to holiness. When you were slaves of sin, you were free from righteousness. (6:16–20)

Saint Paul continues the theme in the next chapter where he describes the interior battles faced by all who have allowed themselves to have been sold as slaves to sin (see Rom 7:14). Those in this state experience even the slightest of virtues as a colossal labor and quickly resile therefrom.

INDEBTEDNESS: "FORGIVE US OUR DEBTS AS WE FORGIVE OUR DEBTORS" (MATT 6:12)

The idea of sin as a state of indebtedness is relatively late, certainly postexilic. There seems to be no evidence of the use of the Hebrew equivalents to the Aramaic *choba'*, meaning "debt."[4] The idea of sin as debt suggested the dangerous conclusion that it could, somehow, be repaid. As a more general notion of sinfulness gave way before the idea of particular sins, the idea appeared that once a sin had been committed, a debt was incurred, for which compensation could be made by appropriate good works. Joachim Jeremias describes this attitude in relation to the Pharisees:

> The idea of merit makes sin innocuous in that a counter-balance is set against it. Merit compensates for sins. . . . According to a commonly used picture, merit is like capital that accumulates in heaven and is laid up there for the pious. The only important thing is that in the final judgment merits should outweigh transgressions.[5]

In the Lord's Prayer, when Jesus says, "Acquit us of our debts as we acquit those who are indebted to us," he is thinking in terms of a debt that is utterly beyond our means to repay, as in the parable of the Unforgiving Servant (see Matt 18:21–35).[6] The only way to be rid of the debt of sin is for God to abolish it.

DEATH: "THE STING OF DEATH IS SIN" (1 COR 15:56)

The narrative of Adam and Eve, composed to offer an explanation for the woes inherent in the human condition, locates the origin of

---

[4] According to the *New English Bible*, Ezek 18:7 is "unintelligible," though other versions attempt to translate it. The corresponding Greek lexeme *'opheilein* occurs a mere twenty-seven times in the Septuagint, thirteen of these are in the Apocrypha.

[5] Joachim Jeremias, *New Testament Theology: Part One, The Proclamation of Jesus* (London: SCM Press, 1971), 147–48.

[6] The Vulgate Latin and all the earliest English translations of the Bible translate the Greek *opheilemata* as "debts"—thus Wycliffe (1380), the Geneva Bible (1562), the Douai-Rheims Version (1582), and the King James Version (1611). The translation as "trespasses" (transgressions, understood as breaches of the law) comes from the *Book of Common Prayer* in 1602.

all our troubles in the disobedience of these ancient progenitors. As an effect of their act, death became part of the human story. This begins a long tradition of seeing death as the logical consequence of sin. In other words, there is the conviction that sin, in all its forms, is ultimately life-denying. The more serious the sin, the deadlier the consequences. As Saint Paul later asserts, "The salary of sin is death" (Rom 6:23).[7] Deuteronomy exhorts us to choose life over death (30:15, 19), which the Fourth Evangelist interprets in terms of adhering to the word of Jesus (John 8:51–52). In that context, the choice of life amounts to receiving the Word made flesh, who becomes for us both resurrection and life.

* * *

As these images show—as do others such as shame and nakedness, hunger and thirst, and many more—the biblical notion of sin regarded it as a crippling element in human life, causing suffering, misery, conflict, and ultimately death. Contrary to the popular notion that committing sin is a matter of enjoying oneself and having fun, Saint Augustine makes the point that sin is not something that enhances life but rather is often accompanied by deep unhappiness; it is "committed by people weeping and groaning in distress."[8] Human experience cannot be understood fully without a solid appreciation of the nature and consequences of human sinfulness.

Unfortunately, sin has fallen prey to moralists. Instead of concentrating their attention on the universal attraction to evil and the ongoing and cumulative effects of wrongdoing, moralists

---

[7] The connection between sin and death is often made in the Epistle to the Romans. Thus, for example, 5:12, 5:21, 6:16, 6:21, 6:23, 7:13, 8:2.

[8] In writing against the Pelagians, Augustine is noting that, although many sins have their origin in pride, not all are committed *proudly*. "Multa enim peccata per superbiam committuntur, sed neque omnia superbe fiunt, quae perperam fiunt, certe a nescientibus, certe ab infirmis, certe plerumque a flentibus et gementibus." *De natura et gratia* 29.33; *Patrologia Latina* 44.263.

love to limit themselves to the minute analysis of particular actions. Sin is seen to be a matter of the things that we do or omit to do, rather than an expression or manifestation of the truth of our existential status. In the postexilic period, when the Pentateuch was compiled, there occurred a new emphasis on sin as law-breaking. The culture that emanated from a concentration on the Ten Commandments had the effect of making sin seem to consist in discrete and concrete actions, observable from the outside. These particular actions could then be compared with the commandments of the Torah and the 613 regulations that translated the Decalogue into practical measures.[9] These breaches of social norms are visible: they can be observed, analyzed, and judged. The deeper and cumulative effect of the preexisting state of sinfulness is less obvious and, as a result, has been often overlooked.

As the Gospels present them, the Pharisees seem to have fallen prey to this hyperzealous legalism. They are criticized by Jesus for straining out the gnats while swallowing camels. In particular, their division of sin into greater and lesser categories had as its result a tendency to regard the lesser sins as unimportant. The Pharisees would concentrate on avoiding only those sins that they classified as more serious. As a result, small sins slowly and imperceptibly inflate and become larger sins, while still remaining under the radar. Consciousness of sin fades. The conscience has been blunted:

> It is the pious whom Jesus regards as being in special danger and at a special remove from God: *they do not take sin seriously*. . . . In Pharisaic Judaism, sin is made innocuous by two things: by casuistry and by the idea of merit. Casuistry views the individual sin in isolation. . . . Gradations are made of conscious and unconscious sins,

[9] These include 248 positive obligations and 365 prohibitions. For a listing, see www.chabad.org.

> greater and lesser sins. The main thing is not to commit any greater sin. The result of this casuistry is that sin is not seen as rebellion against God.[10]

There are those who assert that this approach to sin has been triumphant also in the Catholic Church. In the sixth century, Irish monks compiled lists of sins and their appropriate penances. A confessor availing himself of a *Penitential* did not have to involve himself with the deep dynamics of personal sinfulness, but just consulted the book and imposed a penance. Extenuating circumstances or subjective dispositions played little role in measuring the extent of guilt or its punishment. This approach to wrongdoing was more forensic than moral. As a boy, I learned to answer the *Catechism* question "What is sin?" with the words, "Sin is any willful thought, word, deed, or omission, against the law of God." And it was these particular actions that were to be itemized as appropriate material for the sacrament of reconciliation. The trouble is that laundry-list confessions never quite touch the spot.[11] Those who limit sinfulness to the commission of particular sinful acts can say, "If I hadn't done these things, I would not be a sinner. If circumstances had been different, or if I had not been provoked, I would have escaped sin. Apart from these actions I am totally innocent." This is to lose the connection between the inward condition of a person and the outward actions that give expression to the interior reality. It is to mistake the symptoms for the disease. Our sinful state is certainly embodied in our wrongful actions, but it is not limited to them; it preexists them and overflows their boundaries.

Because the first five scriptural books are printed at the front of our Bibles, we sometimes forget that the Pentateuch was

---

[10] Jeremias, *New Testament Theology*, 147.

[11] "And no one ever confessed his whole sin, for every confession remains summary and incomplete." Adrienne von Speyr, *The Farewell Discourses: Meditations on John 13—17* (San Francisco: Ignatius Press, 1987), 40.

compiled after Second Isaiah. The evocation of Israel's sinfulness in Isa 40–55 is less tarnished by later legalism and more intuitive and symbolic in its approach. Above all, it is colored by the conviction that the destruction of Jerusalem and the exiling of its people were the direct consequences of sin. Sin introduces evil and chaos into an otherwise well-ordered life. Once sin has taken up residence, the way is open to utter disaster. The nature of sin, therefore, can be inferred from its effects. Without God, things fall apart—we may well discover this for ourselves. In the case of Israel, the gravity of such apostasy was such that the ongoing existence of the People of the Covenant is in jeopardy because of it.

Among the words in Second Isaiah most frequently translated as "sin" and its synonyms are *chatah* (to miss, to make a mistake, to do wrong), *'awon* (iniquity, guilt, punishment), *pesha'* (transgression, rebellion), and *resha'* (wickedness).[12] As usual, these assigned meanings are generalizations; individual instances often carry particular nuances.

In Second Isaiah, sin is understood as the cumulative rupture of the covenant relationship between God and Israel, from the side of Israel, not from the side of God. Just as righteousness was understood to be the foundation of the well-ordered relationships required for a cohesive community living in accordance with God's *torah*, so sin—in all its forms—was seen as undermining harmonious solidarity with God and within the nation. Breaking faith with God not only threatened Israel's relationship with God, it had consequences for the internal cohesiveness of the nation. This was demonstrated in the division between Judah and the Northern Kingdom. Only one of the twelve tribes survived intact after the Assyrian invasion. On an individual level, sin inevitably leads to a loss of personal integration, to inner inconsistency, to

[12] Thus *chatah*: 40:2, 42:24, 43:24, 43:25, 43:27, 44:22, 53:12; *'awon*: 40:2, 43:24, 50:1, 53:5, 53:6, 53:11; *pesha'*: 43:25, 43:27, 44:22, 46:8, 48:8, 50:1, 53:5, 53:8, 53:12; *resha'*: 48:22, 50:9, 53:9, 54:17, 55:7.

a yawning gap between self-image and reality. In Second Isaiah, there is a certain fluidity in the notion of the sinner; sometimes the term refers to an individual, and sometimes it refers to the people as a whole. "Thy first father hath sinned and thy teachers have sinned against me. Therefore I have profaned the sanctuary, and have made Jacob a curse and Israel a reproach" (43:24). The whole community suffers the consequence of the sins of the few, and in the case of the Servant, one must suffer for the sake of the many. This understanding of the social implications of sin is quite different from our usual emphasis on individual acts of individual persons that will eventually lead to individual penalties for that person. All sin has social repercussions.

The nature of sin is inferred from its consequences. Thus, a sinful life is marked by the absence of God. A phrase that is used often in the Bible is "the hiding of God's face" (54:8). As a result of sin, we have allowed ourselves to move outside the divine sphere: "My way is hidden from the Lord" (40:27). We are on our own. This is not an irreversible state; if God hides, it is for pedagogical reasons: to teach us to give up our delusional autonomy and learn to live in dependence. Often, however, the perceived absence of God is the result of more or less deliberate choices that we have made. "Each of us has gone our own way" (53:6), which has led to disaster. "This people is robbed and spoiled and shall be all snared in dungeons and they shall be hid in prison houses; they shall be for prey, and none shall deliver a spoil, and none shall say, Restore" (42:22).

If God is absent from our lives, it is because we have banished God by our neglectfulness in maintaining contact with the divine presence: "Thou hast not known me" (45:6).

> And thou hast not called upon me, O Jacob, but thou hast wearied me, O Israel. Thou hast not brought me the sheep of thy burnt offerings, neither hast thou honoured me with thy sacrifices. I have not caused thee to serve with an offering, nor wearied thee with incense. Thou

> broughtest me no sweet savour with money, neither hast thou made me drunk with the fat of thy sacrifices, but thou hast made me to serve with thy sins, *and* wearied me with thine iniquities. (Isa 43:22–24)

Even when God repeatedly took the initiative and reached out to Israel, there was no response. "Wherefore came I, and there was no man? I called, and none answered" (50:2). "But when I beheld, there was none: and when I inquired of them, there *was* no counselor, and when I demanded of them, they answered not a word" (41:28). The absence of God, about which Israel complains, is not of God's doing. It is because the people have abandoned God. This is the scenario that Saint Augustine often conjures up: God is not absent from us; we are absent from God—by our own choice.

Sin is forgetfulness of God—writing God out of the script of our lives:

> Thus saith the Lord thy redeemer, the Holy one of Israel, I am the Lord thy God, which teach thee to profit, and lead thee by the way that thou shouldest go. Oh, that thou hadst hearkened to my commandments! then had thy prosperity been as the flood, and thy righteousness as the waves of the sea. Thy seed also had been as the sand, and the fruit of thy body like the gravel thereof: his name should not have been cut off nor destroyed before me. (Isa 48:17–19)

Such forgetfulness is not mere absentmindedness. It is willful. It amounts to rebellion. All the evils that befell the nation are "because I knew that thou art obstinate, and thy neck is an iron sinew, and thy brow brass" (48:4). The disaster inflicted on Israel is intended to destroy its complacency, to become aware of its own neediness and thus be impelled to turn again to God and to call out for help. It is only in such extreme misery that Israel will recognize its need to turn to its Creator and to seek a second chance, a new beginning:

> Therefore now hear, thou that art given to pleasures, and dwellest careless, She saith in her heart, I am and none else: I shall not sit as a widow, neither shall know the loss of children. But these two things shall come to thee suddenly on one day, the loss of children and widowhood; they shall come upon thee in their perfection, for the multitude of thy divinations, and for the great abundance of thine enchanters. For thou hast trusted in thy wickedness; thou hast said, None seeth me. Thy wisdom and thy knowledge, they have caused thee to rebel, and thou hast said in thine heart, I am, and none else. Therefore shall evil come upon thee, and thou shalt not know the morning thereof; destruction shall fall upon thee, which thou shalt not be able to put away: destruction shall come upon thee suddenly, or thou beware. (Isa 47:8–11)

To banish God from our lives—even though we may think of it merely as a temporary sidelining while we attend to other matters—means that we begin to live as if there were no God. Religious rituals, if we persist in them, have no transcendent meaning. They are mere tokens of social compliance. Subjectively, that interior part of human nature that finds nurturance in contact with the spiritual world begins to desiccate. Almost inevitably—despite protestations to the contrary—we begin to seek alternative sources of meaning. For some, this involves the embrace of a quasireligious atheism;[13] for others, it is the mental indolence of

---

[13] As enunciated by John Gray in *Seven Types of Atheism*. For example, he concludes, "If you want to understand atheism and religion, you must forget the popular notion that they are opposites. . . . Contemporary atheism is a continuation of monotheism by other means" (158).

agnosticism. Then there are those who attempt to create a religion for themselves, an example of the *ethelothreskia* referred to in Colossians 2:23. In the time of Second Isaiah, the great substitute and compensation for the abandonment of the austere demands of traditional observance was idolatry.

Second Isaiah is often described as a Book of Consolation, and as we have seen, there is much comfort to be found in its pages. But there is also a persistent challenge to the prevailing practices of ambient paganism: idolatry, superstition, sorcery. The prophet mocks those who put their trust in blocks of stone and parts of trees. Whatever quality these images have comes from the skills of their makers, but the images themselves are immobile; they can do nothing. They cannot intervene to benefit their sectaries. They cannot speak to provide information on what will happen. All the various self-devised and useless rituals are an abomination. Those who practice them come to a bad end; "they will lie down in sorrow" (50:11).

> The workman melteth an image, or the goldsmith beateth it out in gold, or the goldsmith *maketh* silver plates. Doth not the poor choose out a tree that will not rot, for an oblation? he seeketh also unto him a cunning workman, to prepare an image that shall not be moved. (Isa 40:19–20)

> Every man helped his neighbour, and said to his brother, Be strong. So the workman comforted the founder, *and* he that smote with the hammer, him that smote by course, saying, It is ready for the soldering, and he fastened it with nails that it should not be moved. (Isa 41:6–7)

> Stand to your cause, saith the Lord: bring forth your strong reasons saith the King of Jacob. Let them bring them forth, and let them tell us what shall come, let them show the former things what they be, that we may

consider them, and know the latter end of them: either declare us things for to come. Show the things that are to come hereafter, that we may know that ye are gods: yea, do good or do evil, that we may declare it, and behold it together. Behold, ye are of no value, and your making is of naught: man hath chosen an abomination by them. (Isa 41:21–24)

All they that make an image, are vanity, and their delectable things shall nothing profit: and they are their own witnesses, that they see not nor know: therefore they shall be confounded. Who hath made a god, or molten an image, that is profitable for nothing? Behold, all that are of the fellowship thereof, shall be confounded: for the workmen themselves are men: let them all be gathered together, and stand up, yet they shall fear, and be confounded together. The smith taketh an instrument, and worketh in the coals, and fashioneth it with hammers, and worketh it with the strength of his arms, yea, he is an hungered, and his strength faileth, he drinketh no water, and is faint. The carpenter stretcheth forth a line, he fashioneth it with a red thread, he planeth it, and he portrayeth it with the compass, and maketh it after the figure of a man, and according to the beauty of a man, that it may remain in an house. He will hew him down cedars, and take the pine tree and the oak, and taketh courage among the trees of the forest; he planteth a fir tree, and the rain doth nourish it. And man burneth thereof; for he will take thereof, and warm himself: he also kindleth it, and baketh bread, yet he maketh a god, and worshippeth it; he maketh it an idol, and boweth unto it. He burneth the half thereof even in the fire, and upon the half thereof he eateth flesh; he roasteth the roast, and is satisfied; also he warmeth himself and saith, Aha, I am warm, I have been at the fire. And the residue thereof he maketh a god, even his idol; he boweth unto it, and worshippeth and prayeth unto it, and saith, Deliver me; for thou art my god. They have not known, nor understood: for God hath shut their eyes that they cannot see, and their heart, that they cannot understand. And none considereth in his heart, neither is there knowledge nor understanding to say, I have burnt half of it, even in the fire, and have baked bread also upon the coals thereof: I have roasted flesh, and eaten it, and shall I make the residue thereof an abomination? shall I bow to the stock of a tree? He feedeth of ashes: a seduced heart hath deceived him, that he cannot deliver his soul, nor say, Is there not a lie in my right hand? (Isa 44:9–20)

Assemble yourselves, and come: draw near together, ye abject of the Gentiles: they have no knowledge, that set up the wood of their idol, and pray unto a god, that cannot save them. (Isa 45:20)

Bel is bowed down: Nebo is fallen: their idols were upon their beasts, and upon the cattle: they which did bear you, were laden with a weary burden. (Isa 46:1)

Stand now among thine enchanters, and in the multitude of thy soothsayers (with whom thou hast wearied thyself from thy youth) if so be thou mayest have profit, or if so be thou mayest have strength. Thou art wearied in the multitude of thy counsels: let now the astrologers, the stargazers, and prognosticators stand up, and save thee from these things that shall come upon thee. Behold, they shall be as stubble: the fire shall burn them; they shall not deliver their own lives from the power of the flame: there shall be no coals to warm at, nor light to sit by. Thus shall they serve thee, with whom thou hast wearied thee, even

> thy merchants from thy youth; every one shall wander to his own quarters: none shall save thee. (Isa 47:12–15)

> All you, assemble yourselves, and hear: which among them hath declared these things? (Isa 48:14)

Such passages—which most readers would like to delete, as being off-key to the generally positive message of Second Isaiah—represent something like 9 percent of the total content of the book. Clearly, they are not irrelevant digressions. They belong to the heart of the matter. They are important because they set out to explain Israel's complicity in its own disaster. They had forgotten God. That is why bad things happened, not so much as a punishment inflicted on them for their infidelity, but as a necessary consequence of their substituting a self-made "religion" for an authentic relationship with the God of their ancestors. The people became so conditioned by the stupidity they embraced that they lost any sensitivity to truth that might cause them to reassess the choices they had made. As defeat in war, banishment, and enslavement engulfed them, the role of the prophet was to point the finger at their idolatry and other superstitious practices as sources of all their troubles. And to suggest that if a way out of them was to be found, it would be by returning to living and worshiping in accordance with the covenant God had made with them as a pathway to life.[14]

---

[14] To give a banal example of the dynamic at play here: If against sound advice and reason we choose to limit our nutritional intake to fatty foods and sugary drinks, we do thereby not incur any kind of judicial penalty. Our diet is not illegal. We simply become unwell as the necessary consequence of the unhealthy dietary regime we have embraced. We are complicit in and alone responsible for our failing health. The most direct way back to full vitality is to reverse our dietary choices. This means giving priority to rational thought over the dubious pleasure of such eating. In a similar way, moving away from God automatically means that we become submerged in the ultimate meaninglessness of a godless life. If we move away from the fire, we are no longer warmed by its heat.

It is not uncommon for us to interpret passages in the Old Testament that condemn idolatry as being inapplicable to our own situation. Few of us create idols and worship them. It can be observed, however, that those who permanently abandon traditional religious practice will often experience some sort of void in their lives that cries out to be filled. A contemporary example is the common search for a nonreligious spirituality, usually consisting in a meditational practice that does not involve adherence to a demanding organization, or any scrutiny of moral behavior. It seems that at least some people take seriously the astrological readings included in public media; others see tarot cards, crystals, or pyramids as means of access to an invisible world. In many countries, Wicca is expanding and self-avowed witches are clamoring for public recognition as benign practitioners of a legitimate religion. Adopting such alternatives may distract us from the spiritual absence that we may experience as the result of the choices we have made, but they cannot, in the long run, produce any beneficent effect. They are no more effective than a vague agnosticism in changing the heart for the better. In every case, we are choosing a religion that is self-made or of human manufacture in preference to responding to the self-revelation of God. No wonder the outcome is useless. As Henry Longfellow wrote, "Whom the gods would destroy they first make mad."[15] The question asked by the prophet in his final chapter is one that challenges us all: "Why spend money on what is not bread, and your labor on what does not satisfy?" (Isa 55:2).

Second Isaiah is serious in his mockery of pagan religious practices. All sin is stupid because it involves alienation from God and has the potential to lead progressively to incremental distance and thence to total apostasy. Once the covenant relationship is

---

[15] The words are attributed to Prometheus in the poem "The Masque of Pandora" (1875). Thomas Merton was scathing in his criticisms of what he termed "Promethean" spirituality—the idea that by sheer willpower we can force progress in the spiritual life.

weakened to the point where it is unable to sustain itself, its permanent demise seems unavoidable, unless there is a strong unilateral intervention from the side of God. And so the prophet's aim is twofold: to help the people recognize that their plight is the direct result of their abandonment of God, and conversely, the way out of the crisis is to return to God and to fidelity to the covenant relationship. A conversion is necessary. There is no alternative. "There is no rest for the wicked" (48:22).

6

Compassion

Anthropomorphism is a big word that theologians like to hurl into any discourse about God that seems to reduce the divinity to an all-too-human level. For those of us who are human, however, this is the only way that we can affirm anything positive about God. It is easy to say what God is not, but to describe the divine nature in human terms is the only way our minds can begin to grasp something of the infinite reality of God. It demands that we speak more in poetry than in scientific discourse. This is what Jesus did in his parables and metaphors. Often he tried to trigger some sense of the divine mystery by posing questions. In general, he eschewed both law and metaphysics, the two mainstays of the Western church in recent centuries. Obviously, there are limitations in such a right-brain approach. For example, he taught us to address God as "Father"—a word with decidedly definite limitations; yet this was the term that Jesus chose to communicate something of what cannot be fully expressed in human language. It is important that, while we benefit from the insight that comes through the medium of poetry and metaphors, we remain sensitive to the limitation inherent in such usage, and we feed our souls on the richness of the imagery and leave it to the theologians to fret about the inadequacy of this medium.

When we speak of the divine compassion, we are implying not that God suffers when we suffer, but that somehow God intimately understands our pain and is actively concerned to support us and to bring us relief and healing. We are not alone in our suffering.

Israel's emergent monotheistic tradition meant that God was believed to be ultimately responsible for everything that happened. "I am the Lord, and there is none other. I form the light, and create darkness: I make peace, and create evil: I the Lord do all these things" (Isa 45:6–7). Even when secondary agents were seen to be the immediate source of suffering, it was believed that they acted only because God permitted them to do so. When disasters happened, this could only be because God willed it. Furthermore, granted the interpersonal character of Israelite religion, it was assumed that when God allowed such things to happen to Israel, it signified that Israel was no longer the object of divine benevolence but the target of divine wrath. The prophets were not slow to see in these negative events a punishment inflicted by God because Israel had failed to observe its obligations under the covenant. The sinful nation was responsible for its own troubles. It had brought upon itself God's anger, expressed in the withdrawal of divine protection. The result was that Israel was left vulnerable to assault by its predatory neighbors.

In the context of such beliefs, it is not surprising that those to whom Second Isaiah addressed himself should have considered that the disasters that had befallen them were indicative of God's anger and rejection:

> Who gave Jacob for a spoil, and Israel to the robbers? Did not the Lord, because we have sinned against him? for they would not walk in his ways, neither be obedient unto his Law. Therefore he hath poured upon him his fierce wrath, and the strength of battle; and it set him on fire round about, and he knew not, and it burned him up, yet he considered not. (Isa 42:24–25)

> Awake, awake, and stand up, O Jerusalem, which hast drunk at the hand of the Lord the cup of his wrath: thou hast drunken the dregs of the cup of trembling, and wrung them out. There is none to guide her among all her sons, whom she hath brought forth: there is none that taketh her by the hand of all the sons that she hath brought up. These two things are come unto thee: who will lament thee? desolation and destruction and famine, and the sword: by whom shall I comfort thee? Thy sons have fainted, and lie at the head of all the streets as a wild bull in a net, and are full of the wrath of the Lord, and rebuke of thy God. (Isa 51:17–20)

But God is not indifferent and rebukes the chosen instrument of his anger. Babylon will suffer chastisement for the "destructive rage of the oppressor" (51:13) and for the sufferings inflicted on those who, even though they had been unfaithful, remain God's people.

> I was wroth with my people: I have polluted mine inheritance, and given them into thine hand, thou didst show them no mercy, but thou didst lay thy very heavy yoke upon the ancient. (Isa 47:6)

God's choice of Israel was gratuitous, based on no antecedent merit on the part of Israel, and so it will not be abrogated because of failure or fault or any form of fecklessness. It will be subjected to punishment as a means of remediation, but that punishment will come to an end. God's seeming rejection of the people is not permanent; it is a pedagogical tool to bring them to their senses. God moderates the punishment lest in being too zealous in removing the rust, the whole vessel is destroyed:

> For my Name's sake will I defer my wrath, and for my praise, will I refrain it from thee, that I cut thee not off.

> Behold, I have fined thee, but not as silver: I have chosen thee in the furnace of affliction. For mine own sake, for mine own sake will I do it; for how should my Name be polluted? surely I will not give my glory unto another. (Isa 48:9–11)

> Therefore hear now this, thou miserable and drunken, but not with wine. Thus saith thy Lord God, even God that pleadeth the cause of his people, Behold, I have taken out of thine hand the cup of trembling, even the dregs of the cup of my wrath: thou shalt drink it no more. (Isa 51:21–22)

There is passion in God's insistence that what was allowed to happen to Israel was for its ultimate benefit. It was the fruit of an undeviating love and mercy. It was not the result of a truculent outburst, but part of a carefully devised plan to bring Israel to conversion. Every aspect of the disaster was—despite appearances—part of a strategy of ultimate benevolence:

> For the Lord hath called thee, being as a woman forsaken, and afflicted in spirit, and as a young wife when thou wast refused, saith thy God. For a little while have I forsaken thee, but with great compassion will I gather thee. For a moment in mine anger, I hid my face from thee for a little season, but with everlasting mercy have I had compassion on thee, saith the Lord thy redeemer. For this is unto me as the waters of Noah; for as I have sworn that the waters of Noah should no more go over the earth, so have I sworn that I would not be angry with thee, nor rebuke thee. For the mountains shall remove, and the hills shall fall down; but my mercy shall not depart from thee, neither shall the covenant of my peace fall away, saith the Lord, that hath compassion on thee. (Isa 54:6–10)

The prophet is announcing that this season of chastisement has served its purpose and that it is now time for things to change and for Israel to experience the full extent of God's ongoing favor and to return to the land promised to their ancestors:

> Comfort ye, comfort ye my people, will your God say. Speak comfortably to Jerusalem, and cry unto her, that her warfare is accomplished, that her iniquity is pardoned; for she hath received of the Lord's hand double for all her sins. (Isa 40:1–2)

> Surely the Lord shall comfort Zion: he shall comfort all her desolations, and he shall make her desert like Eden, and her wilderness like the garden of the Lord: joy and gladness shall be found therein: praise, and the voice of singing. (51:3)

> I, even I am he that comfort you. Who art thou that thou shouldest fear a mortal man, and the son of man, which shall be made as grass? (Isa 51:12)

> I will go before thee, and make the crooked straight: I will break the brazen doors, and burst the iron bars. And I will give thee the treasures of darkness, and the things hid in secret places, that thou mayest know that I am the Lord which call thee by thy name, even the God of Israel. For Jacob my servant's sake, and Israel mine elect, I will even call thee by thy name, and name thee, though thou hast not known me. I am the Lord, and there is none other; there is no God besides me: I girded thee, though thou hast not known me. (Isa 45:2–5)

A double punishment calls out for a double reversal. The intervention of God would bring about not only deliverance for Israel and return to the land, but also ample retribution on all its enemies and persecutors, and on all who had sought to profit from the withdrawal of Israel's privileges:

> I have a long time held my peace: I have been still and refrained myself; now will I cry like a travailing woman: I will destroy and devour at once. (Isa 42:13)

> Behold, all they that provoke thee, shall be ashamed, and confounded: they shall be as nothing, and they that strive with thee shall perish. Thou shalt seek them and shalt not find them: to wit, the men of thy strife, for they shall be as nothing, and the men that war against thee, as a thing of nought. For I the Lord thy God will hold thy right hand, saying unto thee, Fear not, I will help thee. (Isa 41:11–13)

> I will go before thee, and make the crooked straight: I will break the brazen doors, and burst the iron bars. And I will give thee the treasures of darkness, and the things hid in secret places, that thou mayest know that I am the Lord which call thee by thy name, even the God of Israel. For Jacob my servant's sake, and Israel mine elect, I will even call thee by thy name, and name thee, though thou hast not known me. I am the Lord, and there is none other; there is no God besides me: I girded thee, though thou hast not known me. (Isa 45:2–5)

This text seems to indicate that the work of restoration and the concern for Israel's welfare derive from God's fidelity to their eponymous ancestor. It is not due to any merit on the part of the present generation. They are alienated from God through their sin, and so are not tuned into what is being accomplished on their behalf. In fidelity to the ancient covenant, God acts unilaterally to forgive their sin and restore their fortunes:

> I, even I am he that putteth away thine iniquities for mine own sake, and will not remember thy sins. (Isa 43:25)

This passionate defense of Israel is not merely a momentary response to its ruin; it is the fruit of a long-established relationship guaranteed by covenant. It is as though God has invested so much in the well-being of the people that there can be no question of allowing them to perish completely. God created and formed Israel from its very beginning and has acted as its protector and avenger, its *go'el*:

> Hear ye me, O house of Jacob, and all that remain of the house of Israel, which are born of me from the womb, and brought up of me from the birth. Therefore unto old age, I the same, even I will bear you until the hoary hairs: I have made you: I will also bear you, and I will carry you, and I will deliver you. (Isa 46:3–4)

The Lord will never abandon the people but will accompany them on their journey, giving them preference and priority over every other nation. There is no need to be afraid, because their God will accompany them in even the most perilous situations. Though the present may seem to be hopeless, the future will witness that all will be well, even though the people lack the most basic means to save themselves:

> But now thus saith the Lord, that created thee, O Jacob: and he that formed thee, O Israel, Fear not: for I have redeemed thee: I have called thee by thy name, thou art mine. When thou passest through the waters, I will be with thee, and through the floods, that they do not overflow thee. When thou walkest through the very fire, thou shalt not be burnt, neither shall the flame kindle upon thee. For I am the Lord thy God, the holy one of Israel, thy Savior: I gave Egypt for thy ransom, Ethio-

> pia, and Seba for thee. Because thou wast precious in my sight, and thou wast honorable, and I loved thee, therefore will I give man for thee, and people for thy sake. Fear not, for I am with thee: I will bring thy seed from the East, and gather thee from the West. I will say to the North, Give: and to the South, Keep not back: bring my sons from far, and my daughters from the ends of the earth. Everyone shall be called by my Name: for I created him for my glory, formed him and made him. I will bring forth the blind people, and they shall have eyes, and the deaf, and they shall have ears. (Isa 43:1–8)

This hope is grounded in the fact that, from its first formation, Israel has been assigned a mission. Summoned, supported, and sustained, Servant Israel is intended to be the catalyst by which all nations will be liberated from their prevailing darkness and brought into the light of God's self-revelation. The completion of this mission is essential for the full manifestation of God's glory. To this end, Israel is not allowed to fail:

> I the Lord have called thee in righteousness, and will hold thine hand, and I will keep thee, and give thee for a covenant of the people, and for a light of the Gentiles, That thou mayest open the eyes of the blind, and bring out the prisoners from the prison: and them that sit in darkness, out of the prison house. (Isa 42:6–7)

> Thus saith the Lord, In an acceptable time have I heard thee, and in a day of salvation have I helped thee: and I will preserve thee, and will give thee for a covenant of the people, that thou mayest raise up the earth, and obtain the inheritance of the desolate heritages: That thou mayest say to the prisoners, Go forth; and to them that are in darkness, Show yourselves; they shall feed in the ways, and their pastures shall be in all the tops of the hills. They

> shall not be hungry, neither shall they be thirsty, neither shall the heat smite them, nor the sun, for he that hath compassion on them, shall lead them; even to the springs of water shall he drive them. (Isa 49:8–10)

The source of this tender care is God's compassion for all. As a result, all the nations will come to be included in Israel's covenant. Darkness and enslavement, hunger, thirst and burning heat will all come to an end. It is as though there will be a new creation in which all the tangible effects of sin are abolished.

Meanwhile, there is work for the people to accomplish. First, they need to overcome their hesitation about accepting the truth of the prophetic message. The task of return and restoration will be great. To take the initial steps, they need to overcome their doubt in the power of God to accomplish what has been proposed. Also, the hesitation, which expresses itself in foreboding and fear, must be left aside. Then they need to be open to receive from God the strength to cooperate in the spectacular events that God will bring about:

> Fear thou not, for I am with thee: be not afraid, for I am thy God: I will strengthen thee, and help thee, and will sustain thee with the right hand of my justice. (Isa 41:10)

> Fear not thou worm, Jacob, and ye men of Israel: I will help thee, saith the Lord, and thy redeemer the holy One of Israel. (Isa 41:14)

> But he giveth strength unto him that fainteth, and unto him that hath no strength, he increaseth power. Even the young men shall faint, and be weary, and the young men shall stumble and fall. But they that wait upon the Lord, shall renew their strength: they shall lift up the wings, as the eagles: they shall run, and not be weary, and they shall walk and not faint. (Isa 40:29–31)

Throughout Second Isaiah appears the recurrent theme of the divine tenderness. This theme is expressed with a clarity and eloquence that rival almost anything else in the Old Testament, creating strong and memorable images in the reader's mind: the shepherd holding the vulnerable lamb to his bosom, the mother nursing her child, the husband whose love outweighs the infidelity of his spouse, and the God of the cosmic covenant whose fidelity is total:

> He shall feed his flock like a shepherd: he shall gather the lambs with his arm, and carry them in his bosom, and shall guide them with young. (Isa 40:11)

> But Zion said, The Lord hath forsaken me, and my Lord hath forgotten me. Can a woman forget her child, and not have compassion on the son of her womb? though they should forget, yet will I not forget thee. Behold, I have graven thee upon the palm of mine hands: thy walls are ever in my sight. Thy builders make haste: thy destroyers and they that made thee waste, are departed from thee. (Isa 49:14–17)

> Fear not: for thou shalt not be ashamed, neither shalt thou be confounded: for thou shalt not be put to shame: yea, thou shalt forget the shame of thy youth, and shalt not remember the reproach of thy widowhood anymore. For he that made thee, is thine husband, (whose name is the Lord of hosts) and thy redeemer the holy One of Israel, shall be called the God of the whole world. For the Lord hath called thee, being as a woman forsaken, and afflicted in spirit, and as a young wife when thou wast refused, saith thy God. For a little while have I forsaken thee, but with great compassion will I gather thee. For a moment in mine anger, I hid my face from thee for a little season, but with everlasting mercy have I had compassion on thee, saith the Lord thy redeemer. For this is

> unto me as the waters of Noah; for as I have sworn that the waters of Noah should no more go over the earth, so have I sworn that I would not be angry with thee, nor rebuke thee. For the mountains shall remove, and the hills shall fall down; but my mercy shall not depart from thee, neither shall the covenant of my peace fall away, saith the Lord, that hath compassion on thee. (Isa 54:4–10)

The prophet's task of proclaiming good news is not based on any denial that the present situation is anything but bad. Nor does he gloss over the fact that the responsibility for the decline in Israel's fortunes is its own. It has drifted away from God, embraced the practices of pagan religion, and left aside its obligations under the covenant. Second Isaiah affirms all this unambiguously. Only when Israel has been found guilty is the sentence of acquittal pronounced. God will intervene and, acting through secondary agents, will bring about the restoration of Israel and the promise of a glorious future. The initiative is God's, who alone will ensure that this new creation will be brought to fulfillment.

For the moment, the obligation on God's people is that they receive in faith the good news that the prophet has proclaimed. They must allow the hope that it inspires to energize and sustain them in the next phase of the journey with God, certain that the promises made to them will not be voided:

> Incline your ears, and come unto me: hear, and your soul shall live, and I will make an everlasting covenant with you, even the sure mercies of David. (Isa 55:3)

The gift of the prophet is hope—a hope based not on what the prophet can himself provide, but a hope that is built on the acceptance of the all-wise providence of God, who is able to write straight on crooked lines. This is a hope that is sustained by an appreciation of the overwhelming and unconditional love that God has for his people and, ultimately, for all the inhabitants of the world:

> Why sayest thou, O Jacob, and speakest O Israel, My way is hid from the Lord, and my judgment is passed over of my God? Knowest thou not? or hast thou not heard, that the everlasting God, the Lord hath created the ends of the earth? he neither fainteth, nor is weary: there is no searching of his understanding. But he giveth strength unto him that fainteth, and unto him that hath no strength, he increaseth power. Even the young men shall faint, and be weary, and the young men shall stumble and fall. But they that wait upon the Lord, shall renew their strength: they shall lift up the wings, as the eagles: they shall run, and not be weary, and they shall walk and not faint. (Isa 40:27–31)

Two words are used to describe what we might term the "subjective attitude" of God toward Israel and, beyond Israel, to humanity itself.

CHESED (MERCY)

This term is found some 248 times in the Old Testament, including 127 times in the Book of Psalms. It is often translated simply as "mercy." This is the easiest option. Miles Coverdale created a new translation for it as "lovingkindness," and the Revised Standard Version often renders it as "steadfast love." It points to a rich and complex reality. As used throughout the Bible, *chesed* needs to be understood in terms of the abiding connectedness of God and Israel resulting from the covenant, expressed in an active fidelity to the obligations assumed in that relationship. The term is used relatively rarely in Second Isaiah, though the sense of it strongly pervades the entire book. Of the four occurrences, the most significant are these: "For a moment in mine anger, I hid my face from thee for a little season, but with everlasting *mercy* have I had compassion on thee, saith the Lord thy redeemer" (54:8), and "For the mountains shall remove, and the hills shall fall down; but my *mercy* shall not depart from thee, neither shall the covenant of my peace fall away, saith the Lord, that hath compassion on thee" (54:10). In both cases, the enduring nature of *chesed* is emphasized.

> Everything that is said focuses on what Yahweh does for Israel and the individual worshipper. The history of Yahweh's people, past present and future, the life of the individual Israelite—in fact the entire world—is the stage for the demonstration of Yahweh's kindness. Yahweh has decided in favor of Israel; he has promised life, care, alleviation of distress, and preservation—indeed, he has filled the whole earth with his kindness. He has thus granted fellowship with him to his people, to all mankind, to the whole world. And this act, like the promise of future help and fellowship, is characterized by permanence, constancy, and reliability. This is what Israel and the individual Israelite hear through Yahweh's word, including the word spoken through the mouth of his prophets.[1]

RACHAM (TO SHOW COMPASSION)

The meaning of this lexeme is influenced by the fact that it includes the notion of the maternal womb, as in Isa 46:3.[2] There is a note of tenderness about it. God's compassion extends even to the wicked (55:7). The divine compassion is represented as more than a feeling; it is active. Often the reference depicts God's response to hardship. Not content merely to grieve over the calamitous circumstances into which Israel has allowed itself to

---

[1] G. Johannes Botterweck and Helmer Ringgren, eds., s.v. "*chesed*," *Theological Dictionary of the Old Testament*, vol. 5, trans. David E. Green (Grand Rapids: Eerdmans, 1986), 62.

[2] Here it is used alongside another word for "womb," *beten*, which appears at 44:2, 44:24, 48:8, 49:1, 49:5, and 49:15.

be drawn, it sets about improving the situation and restoring the people to the previous state.[3]

> Thus saith the Lord, In an acceptable time have I heard thee, and in a day of salvation have I helped thee: and I will preserve thee, and will give thee for a covenant of the people, that thou mayest raise up the earth, and obtain the inheritance of the desolate heritages: That thou mayest say to the prisoners, Go forth; and to them that are in darkness, Show yourselves; they shall feed in the ways, and their pastures shall be in all the tops of the hills. They shall not be hungry, neither shall they be thirsty, neither shall the heat smite them, nor the sun, for he that hath *compassion* on them, shall lead them; even to the springs of water shall he drive them. And I will make all my mountains, as a way, and my paths shall be exalted. Behold, these shall come from far: and lo, these from the North and from the West, and these from the land of Sinim. Rejoice, O heavens; and be joyful, O earth; burst forth into praise, O mountains; for God hath comforted his people, and will have *mercy* upon his afflicted. But Zion said, The Lord hath forsaken me, and my Lord hath forgotten me. Can a woman forget her child, and not have *compassion* on the son of her womb? though they should forget, yet will I not forget thee. Behold, I have graven thee upon the palm of mine hands: thy walls are ever in my sight. (Isa 49:8–16)

The benevolence of God is shown also in other metaphors. "He shall feed his flock like a shepherd: he shall gather the lambs with his arm, and carry them in his bosom, and shall guide them with young" (40:11). The Lord will accompany the people (43:2–5), guiding them by the hand (41:6, 41:9, 41:13,

---

[3] See 54:6–10, quoted above.

42:6, 49:10) carrying them (46:3–4) and giving them strength (40:29–31). God is their *go'el*, their kinsman, their redeemer, their protector and avenger (cf. 41:14, 43:1, 43:14, 44:6, 44:22, 44:23, 44:24, 47:4, 48:17, 48:20, 49:7, 49:26, 51:10, 52:3, 52:9, 54:5) who forgives their failings (43:25, 44:21) and who will be their comfort (41:11–13, 51:3, 51:12, 52:9) and their lifelong support (46:4).

God's love will lead the people back to the land of their ancestors and reestablish them there in an enduring peace. The word *shalom* may, perhaps, be more materially translated as "completeness," "prosperity," or "well-being." It is God who is the ultimate and only source of an inviolate peace: "I make peace and create evil" (45:7). This implies that genuine peace is the effect of our being acted upon by God, presupposing that we are willing to receive the gift. In contrast, coming face-to-face with God will bring about a complete loss of peace in those whose dispositions are wrong. Encounter with the absolute truth of God reveals our true state. "There is no peace for the wicked, says the Lord" (48:22). Because of the firm "covenant of peace" (54:10) established with Israel, "much peace shall be to thy children" (54:13). The way to peace is clear: fulfilling the obligations of the covenant. "Oh, that thou hadst hearkened to my commandments! then had thy peace been as the flood and thy righteousness as the waves of the sea" (48:18). Fidelity to *torah* will mean that Israel can be certain that deliverance will come: "Therefore ye shall go out with joy, and be led forth with peace" (55:12).

By God's intervention a great reversal takes place. Where there had been desolation and mourning, now there will rebuilding and rejoicing:

> Surely the Lord shall comfort Zion: he shall comfort all her desolations, and he shall make her desert like Eden, and her wilderness like the garden of the Lord: joy and gladness shall be found therein: praise, and the voice of singing. (Isa 51:3)

Peace and prosperity involve not only the end of hostilities but the elimination of potential disrupters of harmony:

> Behold, all they that provoke thee, shall be ashamed, and confounded: they shall be as nothing, and they that strive with thee shall perish. Thou shalt seek them and shalt not find them: to wit, the men of thy strife, for they shall be as nothing, and the men that war against thee, as a thing of nought. For I the Lord thy God will hold thy right hand, saying unto thee, Fear not, I will help thee. (Isa 41:11–13)

This assurance is grounded on the disparity between God and any fleshly adversaries. No matter how strong human despots appear, they remain mortal and easily vincible by the Lord:

> I, even I am he that comfort you. Who art thou that thou shouldest fear a mortal man, and the son of man, which shall be made as grass? (Isa 51:12)

The outcome is certain. Peace and prosperity forever. They are in God's gift and they will be made available when Jerusalem is reclaimed:

> O ye desolate places of Jerusalem, be glad and rejoice together, for the Lord hath comforted his people: he hath redeemed Jerusalem. (Isa 52:9)

The return of God's people to their land and the restoration of Jerusalem are the concrete manifestations of God's glory, which is no less than the self-manifestation of the infinite compassion that God has for Israel and for all humanity: a compassion that overlooks infidelity and brings healing and resolution to sin and its effects, and offers the promise of a more abundant life.

7

Awake!

Second Isaiah proclaimed a loving God who was willing to intervene in earthly affairs in order to reverse the disasters wrought by Israel's infidelity. As such, the prophet's message can be translated into our own idiom as a promise to deliver us from the state of alienation from God that has been built up by our personal and collective history of wrong choices. The prophet speaks a truth that transcends the parameters of the space and time in which it was first delivered. The word is addressed also to us.

It is important, however, that we do not use God's unconditional acceptance and love as a pretext for inaction. The message of Second Isaiah is not aimed at producing a state of pious indolence; it is a call to action. The opening words of the prophet make this clear:

> Prepare ye the way of the Lord: make straight in the desert a path for our God. Every valley shall be exalted, and every mountain and hill shall be made low; and the crooked shall be straight, and the rough places plain. (Isa 40:3–4)

Israel is not inactive; it has a vigorous role to play in eliminating the obstacles to its own restoration and in promoting the Lord's purpose on earth:

> Behold, I will make thee a roller, and a new threshing instrument having teeth: thou shalt thresh the mountains, and bring them to powder, and shalt make the hills as chaff. Thou shalt fan them, and the wind shall carry them away, and the whirlwind shall scatter them: and thou shalt rejoice in the Lord, and shalt glory in the holy One of Israel. (Isa 41:15–16)

The promise of divine intervention is unequivocal, but it demands that we remain vigilant, ready to exploit the opportunity offered by the moment of grace. We need to get busy. Our earthworks are not productive of the deliverance for which we hope. They are, rather, expressions of our confidence in the impending action of God. Being actively involved demonstrates that this hope is well-established. No one willingly invests energy in a task that is unlikely to produce fruits:

> He shall not fail nor be discouraged till he have set judgment in the earth: and the isles shall wait for his Law. . . . I the Lord have called thee in righteousness, and will hold thine hand, and I will keep thee, and give thee for a covenant of the people, and for a light of the Gentiles, That thou mayest open the eyes of the blind, and bring out the prisoners from the prison: and them that sit in darkness, out of the prison house. (Isa 41:4–7)

The first task is to raise oneself from the state of somnolence and from drunken stupor and to put aside the cup of wrath. The situation of the exiles in Babylon was dire, but not hopeless. The first stage in the spiritual journey is this moment of awakening, whether it be from depressed hopelessness or from the comfortable languor of complacency. Before anything else we have to wake up:

> Awake, awake, and stand up, O Jerusalem, which hast drunk at the hand of the Lord the cup of his wrath:

> thou hast drunken the dregs of the cup of trembling, and wrung them out. There is none to guide her among all her sons, whom she hath brought forth: there is none that taketh her by the hand of all the sons that she hath brought up. These two things are come unto thee: who will lament thee? desolation and destruction and famine, and the sword: by whom shall I comfort thee? Thy sons have fainted, and lie at the head of all the streets as a wild bull in a net, and are full of the wrath of the Lord, and rebuke of thy God. Therefore hear now this, thou miserable and drunken, but not with wine. Thus saith thy Lord God, even God that pleadeth the cause of his people, Behold, I have taken out of thine hand the cup of trembling, even the dregs of the cup of my wrath: thou shalt drink it no more. But I will put it into their hand that spoil thee, which have said to thy soul, Bow down that we may go over, and thou hast laid thy body as the ground, and as the streets to them that went over. Arise, arise: put on thy strength, O Zion: put on the garments of thy beauty, O Jerusalem, the holy City: for henceforth there shall no more come into thee the uncircumcised and the unclean. Shake thyself from the dust, arise, and sit down, O Jerusalem: loose the bands of thy neck, O thou captive daughter Zion. For thus saith the Lord, Ye were sold for naught; therefore shall ye be redeemed without money. (Isa 51:17—52:3)

The call to mindfulness that the prophet addressed to the exiles is one that may be appropriately addressed to God's people in every age. The danger of being lulled into a lethal lethargy is always present, and such indolence is one of the most serious inhibitors of spiritual progress at every stage of development. Listen to the words of a twelfth-century Cistercian monk, Isaac of Stella:

> Let us keep awake, then, brothers, and be on our guard most specially against the plague of spiritual laziness that comes usually of immature self-assurance and infects even such as really have made some progress. They tell themselves that, having overcome all evil tendencies, they may lie down to rest in all safety, with nothing to terrify them. In the case of the less advanced, the fact that their bodily needs are taken care of by others leaves them, so they think, nothing further to do.[1]

The reason for this initial summons is that even though the grace of God is all powerful, its efficacy is limited by our willingness to welcome it. For this we must be awake, alert, and receptive. Desire goes before the gift and so, as a kind of preamble to the overt operation of grace, desire is kindled in the heart. As we saw in an earlier chapter, desire is composed of two complementary motions: one is to reach beyond the prevailing situation into the realm of the presently unattainable; the other is to experience a profound and generalized dissatisfaction with the status quo. Very often, it is the dissatisfaction that first comes to the surface of consciousness.

The first task that the prophet enjoins on the exiles is to use their heads. To begin, they must recognize the utter stupidity of idolatry (cf. 40:19–20, 41:6–7, 41:21–24, 44:9–20, 45:20, 46:1, 47:12–15, 48:14, 50:11). In contrast, he repeatedly reminds them of the omnipotence of God. As we have seen, the transcendence of Israel's God is a major theme in Second Isaiah. As Creator of all, God is uncaused and unconditioned (cf. 40:12–14, 40:21–26). If proof of this be needed, a survey of Israel's history can be made. God is not inactive in the events that take place in space and time. Since everything that happens is controlled by God, it is possible for them to be announced long before they occur. Israel's

---

[1] Isaac of Stella, *Sermons on the Christian Year: Volume One* (Kalamazoo, MI: Cistercian Publications, 1979), 14:10, 116.

God is the Lord of history. While the dispirited exiles remember that nothing is impossible for God, there will be a foundation for hope:

> Remember the former things of old: for I am God, and there is none other God, and there is nothing like me, Which declare the last thing from the beginning, and from of old: the things that were not done, saying, My counsel shall stand, and I will do whatsoever I will. (Isa 46:9–10)

The exodus is a significant image in the thought of the prophet (cf. 40:3–5, 41:17–20, 42:14–16, 43:1–3, 43:16–21, 48:20–21, 49:8–12, 51:9–11, 52:11–12, 55:12–13). Just as God had liberated Israel from the tyranny of Egypt, with a mighty hand and an outstretched arm, so these same weapons will be deployed against Babylon, and Israel will be liberated to cross the desert and make its home in the land promised to their ancestors. So now it is God whom the prophet is attempting to rouse. God seems to sleep if there seems to be no response to Israel's distress, even though the sleep is Israel's, not God's. God may be said to wake up when Israel changes its stance and is prepared to accept the hope and the help that are always in the offing:

> Rise up, Rise up, and put on strength, O arm of the Lord: rise up as in the old time in the generations of the world. Art not thou the same, that hath cut Rahab, and wounded the dragon? Art not thou the same, which hath dried the Sea, even the waters of the great deep, making the depth of the sea a way for the redeemed to pass over? Therefore the redeemed of the Lord shall return, and come with joy unto Zion, and everlasting joy shall be upon their head: they shall obtain joy and gladness: and sorrow and mourning shall flee away. (Isa 51:9–11)

Israel will "go out" from Babylon, just as previously the people were able to "go out" from Egypt. A "way" or a "road" (*derek*) will be made for them:

> Thus saith the Lord which maketh a way in the Sea, and a path in the mighty waters. When he bringeth out the chariot and horse, the army and the power lie together, and shall not rise, they are extinct, and quenched as tow. Remember ye not the former things, neither regard the things of old. Behold, I do a new thing: now shall it come forth: shall you not know it? I will even make a way in the desert, and floods in the wilderness. The wild beasts shall honor me, the dragons and the ostriches, because I gave water in the desert, and floods in the wilderness to give drink to my people, even to mine elect. This people have I formed for myself: they shall show forth my praise. (Isa 43:16–21)

This is, of course, poetic hyperbole. Ostriches never did get the chance to dance with dragons. The eventual act of deliverance would be much more pedestrian, and the resettlement in the land would be bedeviled with difficulties. The prophet is exaggerating in order to gain the attention of the exiles, speaking to the heart of Jerusalem (cf. 40:2) rather than proffering a detailed description of what is to come. His message is quite simple. The events surrounding the exodus should give the people confidence that God has both the will and the power to deliver them from Babylon. Modern readers need to keep reminding themselves that this was more than a promise; it actually happened.

The message is a call to pay attention—in the language later used by Deuteronomy: to remember, to bring to mind, to keep in mind. In this situation, waking up means learning what to remember and what to forget, sorting through the mental confusion that befogs reality and keeping before one's eyes the most important truths:

> Remember ye not the former things, neither regard the things of old. Behold, I do a new thing: now shall it come forth: shall you not know it? (Isa 43:18–19)

> Put me in remembrance: let us be judged together: count thou that thou mayest be justified. (Isa 43:26)

> Remember these (O Jacob and Israel) for thou art my servant: I have formed thee; thou art my servant: O Israel forget me not. (Isa 44:21)

> Remember this, and be ashamed: bring it again to mind, O you transgressors. Remember the former things of old: for I am God, and there is none other God, and there *is* nothing like me. (Isa 46:8–9)

Forgetfulness and alienation from God lead ineluctably to disaster, and as long as unmindfulness continues, it serves as an inhibitor to envisaging any creative steps to extricate from the morass. By projecting onto God one's own coldness, it will seem that the rupture of the relationship comes from God's side. In our delusion we remain, as always, blameless in our own sight:

> Zion said, The Lord hath forsaken me, and my Lord hath forgotten me. (Isa 49:14)

It is not God who has forgotten us, but we who have forgotten God:

> Thou didst not set thy mind to these things, neither didst thou remember the latter end thereof. (Isa 47:7)

Remaining mindful of the goodness of God allows one to draw more deeply from that life-giving source. Fear is banished, and all the negativity brought on by alienation from God can be banished from consciousness. Shame and reproach belong to the past. This memory of the wonderful deeds of God provides motivation for creative endeavor in the present.

> Fear not: for thou shalt not be ashamed, neither shalt thou be confounded: for thou shalt not be put to shame: yea, thou shalt forget the shame of thy youth, and shalt not remember the reproach of thy widowhood anymore. (Isa 54:4)

Part of this growth in understanding is a sharper self-awareness, in particular, the sober recognition of complicity in one's downfall. The later injunction of Haggai reveals an essential part of prophetic proclamation: "Consider how things have gone with you" (1:5). Second Isaiah has similar imperatives. Look where your apostasy has led you: war, defeat, plunder, devastation, ruin, captivity, exile, and affliction. The significant step to be taken is to recognize that all this is the result of Israel's turning away from God. "Behold, for your iniquities are ye sold, and because of your transgressions is your mother forsaken" (50:1). This is why the nation is lashed by storms (54:11) and thorn bushes and briars have invaded once-arable land (55:13).

Having woken from the sleep of forgetfulness, it is time to respond actively to the summons from God. Like Jeremiah (cf. 51:6), Second Isaiah calls on the people to embark on a bold exodus from Babylon and, under the guiding hand of God, to make their way back to their ancestral land:

> Go ye out of Babel: flee ye from the Chaldeans with a voice of joy: tell and declare this: show it forth to the end of the earth: say ye, The Lord hath redeemed his servant Jacob. And they were not thirsty: he led them through the wilderness: he caused the waters to flow out of the rock for them: for he clave the rock and the water gushed out. (Isa 48:20–21)

> Depart, depart ye: go ye out from thence, and touch no unclean thing, go out of the midst of her, be ye clean, that bear the vessels of the Lord. For ye shall not go out with haste, nor depart by fleeing away: but the Lord will go before you, and the God of Israel will gather you together. (Isa 52:11–12)

The prophet has recognized the signs of the times and declares that the season of tribulation is over and an era of salvation dawns:

> Thus saith the Lord, In an acceptable time have I heard thee, and in a day of salvation have I helped thee: and I will preserve thee, and will give thee for a covenant of the people, that thou mayest raise up the earth, and obtain the inheritance of the desolate heritages: That thou mayest say to the prisoners, Go forth; and to them that are in darkness, Show yourselves; they shall feed in the ways, and their pastures shall be in all the tops of the hills. They shall not be hungry, neither shall they be thirsty, neither shall the heat smite them, nor the sun, for he that hath compassion on them, shall lead them; even to the springs of water shall he drive them. And I will make all my mountains, as a way, and my paths shall be exalted. (Isa 49:8–12)

As is often the case with those enduring chronic hardship, there is an unwillingness to believe that the situation can be remedied. Perhaps there is also a fear of the unknown, being of the opinion that the devil you know is better than the one you don't. The people have to be jolted out of their lethal torpor: to hear the promises, to accept the promises, and decisively to act on the promises:

> Hear me ye stubborn hearted, that are far from justice. I bring near my justice: it shall not be far off, and my salva-

> tion shall not tarry: for I will give salvation in Zion, and my glory unto Israel. (Isa 46:12–13)

> Look unto me, and ye shall be saved: all the ends of the earth shall be saved: for I am God, and there *is* none other. (Isa 46:12)

Ancient commentators like to link the name Babylon with the narrative of the Tower of Babel (cf. Gen 11:1–9), interpreting the name to mean "confusion." This was understood as the mental darkness caused by allowing carnal passions to run riot.[2] An important stage at the beginning of the spiritual journey is to instill some clarity into the mental processes, so that we are able to see our lives as they are, to name our deficiencies, and progressively to identify and neutralize our negative tendencies. Saint Aelred of Rievaulx outlines a strategy of escape: "Flee from the midst of Babylon":

> Now let each one of you think how we were in that spiritual Babylon, how we were afraid, how we were confounded, how much confusion was in the mind of each one of us when on one side anger disturbed us and on another we were constrained by cupidity; here lust burned and, there, envy twisted us out of shape. Before we have consummated a pleasure, we burn with desire, but after its consummation we are wearied by disgust. Out of this confusion God is calling us saying, "Flee from the midst of Babylon."[3]

---

[2] See Rom 1:21: "For this reason, although they knew God, they did not glorify him or give thanks and so they became futile in their thinking and their unintelligent hearts were darkened." As Second Isaiah remarks concerning the makers of idols, "They have not known, nor understood: for God hath shut their eyes that they cannot see, and their heart, that they cannot understand. And none considereth in his heart" (44:18–19).

[3] Aelred of Rievaulx, *Sermones* 82.4; *Corpus Christianorum: Continuatio Mediaevalis IIB*, 334.

The work of salvation will be characterized by two processes: liberation from captivity and regathering in freedom. The scattered and disgraced remnants of Israel will be regathered in order to give rise to a vast multitude of descendants: "Assemble yourselves, and come: draw near together, ye abject of the Gentiles" (Isa 45:20). For this rebirth to happen, the captives must be liberated from the constraints that their bondage imposes on them. If they allow God's intervention to do its work, the people are promised freedom and a generative future:

> Fear not, for I am with thee: I will bring thy seed from the East, and gather thee from the West. I will say to the North, Give: and to the South, Keep not back: bring my sons from far, and my daughters from the ends of the earth. Everyone shall be called by my Name: for I created him for my glory, formed him and made him. I will bring forth the blind people, and they shall have eyes, and the deaf, and they shall have ears. (Isa 43:5–8)

As we, perhaps, know from our own experience, the acceptance of an offer of freedom is often a challenge. Sometimes it is easier to remain as a serf or a victim, tightly holding on to our particular log of grievances as an ongoing excuse for our underachievement. The invitation to come forth from our self-imposed prison is not always welcomed. Our problem is often similar to the exiles to whom it was said, "I knew that thou art obstinate, and thy neck is an iron sinew, and thy brow brass" (48:4). We are reluctant to see our situation from a different perspective and, as a result, are unlikely to heed any admonition to change our ways.

Isaiah 40—55 is clearly a work of strong advocacy. The prophet brings every possible argument to bear in an effort to rouse the exiles from their fatalistic acceptance of their captivity. He scoffs at the lifeless impotence of their captors' gods. He recalls the wonderful deeds done in the past by the Lord and insists that this benevolent power, operative since the moment of creation, remains ready to intervene anew in Israel's favor. In clear language and with poetic eloquence Second Isaiah sets forth grounds for hope, based not on any merit on the people's part, but solely on the gratuitous benevolence of God, and on God's fidelity to the covenant made with Israel's ancestors.

The greatest problem the prophet encounters is the weary apathy of the people to whom he addresses himself. Their hard hearts and stiff necks work together to make them impervious to the good news he announces. Because their minds are closed, the prophet seeks to move them at the level of feeling. In powerful, emotive language he seeks to break through the barrier of rationality and to motivate them to seize the opportunity for liberty that the providence of God is creating for them. It is time for the people to wake up, to open their eyes to what God is causing to happen, and to take whatever steps open before them to return from captivity to freedom in their own land.

8

Deliverance

The English noun "salvation" is commonly used in a religious sense, although the verb "save" has many secular meanings. As it happens, the notion of "salvation," as indicated by the lexeme *yasha'*, is frequent in Second Isaiah.[1] Every other supposed deity (45:20) or idol (46:7) is impotent, as are "the astrologers, the stargazers, and prognosticators" (47:13).[2] "Only God can save (43:11, 49:26). God alone is both savior (*moshi'ek*) and redeemer (*go'el*). In this book, salvation is viewed as something of an absolute: it is never a question of being "saved from" but rather the evocation of a brilliant outcome: "I will also give thee for a light of the Gentiles, that thou mayest be my salvation unto the end of the world" (49:6). Thus, the concept transcends mere rescue from Israel's present predicament; it has a more general and universalist flavor (cf. 45:17, 45:22, 46:13, 49:6, 49:8, 51:6, 51:8, and 52:7–10), a theme taken up strongly in Third Isaiah (Isa 56—66). Seeing salvation as the ultimate and unrestricted benefit often brings the theme into contact with the notion of

[1] 43:3, 43:11, 43:12, 43:15, 45:8, 45:17 (*bis*), 45:20, 45:21, 45:22, 46:7, 46:13 (*bis*), 47:13, 47:15, 49:6, 49:8, 49:26, 51:5, 51:6, 51:8, 52:7, 52:10.

[2] Thus: "I destroy the tokens of the soothsayers, and make them that conjecture, fools, and turn the wise men backward, and make their knowledge foolishness" (44:28).

righteousness (*sedeqah*): "My salvation shall be forever, and my righteousness shall not be abolished" (51:8; see also 45:8, 46:13, and 51:6).

A large portion of Second Isaiah is devoted to presenting the prospect of salvation either through oracles (cf. 41:8–13, 41:14–16, 43:1–4, 43:5–7, 44:1–5, and 54:1–6) or through proclamations (cf. 41:17–20, 42:14–17, 43:16–21, 46:12–13, 49:7–12/13, 49:14–26, 51:1–8, 51:9–16, 54:7–10, 54:11–17, and 55:1–5).[3] These texts are stamped with a certain sureness about future prospects based on the acceptance that God has already begun the process of restoration, and hence there is no longer cause to be afraid. It is, rather, a time for anticipative rejoicing.

The promises conveyed by Second Isaiah are neither vague nor abstract. In the historical context of the period following the deportation of thousands of Jews to Babylon, the message was clear. This situation will come to an end, and the possibility of returning to the land will unfold. For this to happen, several events will have to take place, some of them by the hand of secondary agents. And, unsurprisingly, they will happen in a manner less spectacular and dramatic than the prophetic tirades seem to portray.

In the first phase of liberation, a deadly blow must be aimed at those who are keeping God's people captive. The prophet proclaims the imminent destruction of these enemies. As it happened, Cyrus's entry into Babylon was relatively peaceable, and as was his wont, he enacted a practical policy of leaving things very much as they were under Nabonidus, Babylon's failed final ruler. The prophet's vision of the event was much more dramatic:

> Behold, all they that provoke thee, shall be ashamed, and confounded: they shall be as nothing, and they that strive

---

[3] The list is taken from Anton Schoors, *I Am God Your Saviour: A Form-Critical Study of the Main Genres in Is. XL—LV* (Leiden: Brill, 1973). On the distinction between oracles and proclamations of salvation, see Claus Westermann, *Isaiah 40—66* (London: SCM Press, 1969).

> with thee shall perish. Thou shalt seek them and shalt not find them: to wit, the men of thy strife, for they shall be as nothing, and the men that war against thee, as a thing of nought. For I the Lord thy God will hold thy right hand, saying unto thee, Fear not, I will help thee. Fear not thou worm, Jacob, and ye men of Israel: I will help thee, saith the Lord, and thy redeemer the holy One of Israel. Behold, I will make thee a roller, and a new threshing instrument having teeth: thou shalt thresh the mountains, and bring them to powder, and shalt make the hills as chaff. Thou shalt fan them, and the wind shall carry them away, and the whirlwind shall scatter them: and thou shalt rejoice in the Lord, and shalt glory in the holy One of Israel. (Isa 41:11–16)

Those overpowering forces that seem like mountain bulwarks will quickly be crushed to dust and blown away by the wind. Against seemingly impossible odds, these formidable foes will be reduced to nothing. Even though God has allowed this disaster to occur, it is part of a plan, not the result of inaction. God has allowed Israel to experience the effects of its forsaking of the covenant, but the abandonment by God is temporary. It is strategic and not definitive. The time is fast approaching for God to intervene:

> The Lord shall go forth as a giant; he shall stir up his courage like a man of war: he shall shout and cry, and shall prevail against his enemies. I have a long time held my peace: I have been still and refrained myself; now will I cry like a travailing woman: I will destroy and devour at once. (Isa 42:13–14)

The victory over Israel's captors and the vindication of God's fidelity to the covenant will become manifest in the utter degradation to which the tyrannical overlords will be subject:

> But thus saith the Lord, Even the captivity of the mighty shall be taken away: and the prey of the tyrant shall be delivered: for I will contend with him that contendeth with thee, and I will save thy children, And will feed them that spoil thee, with their own flesh, and they shall be drunken with their own blood, as with sweet wine; and all flesh shall know that I the Lord am thy Saviour and thy Redeemer, the mighty one of Jacob. (Isa 49:25–26)

> For the moth shall eat them up like a garment, and the worm shall eat them like wood: but my righteousness shall be forever, and my salvation from generation to generation. (Isa 51:8)

> Thus saith thy Lord God, even God that pleadeth the cause of his people, Behold, I have taken out of thine hand the cup of trembling, even the dregs of the cup of my wrath: thou shalt drink it no more. But I will put it into their hand that spoil thee, which have said to thy soul, Bow down that we may go over, and thou hast laid thy body as the ground, and as the streets to them that went over. (Isa 51:22–23)

Concretely this involves the destruction of Babylon and the humiliation of its gods, who are unable to defend themselves or the city that has honored them:

> Bel is bowed down: Nebo is fallen: their idols were upon their beasts, and upon the cattle: they which did bear you, were laden with a weary burden. They are bowed down, and fallen together, for they could not rid them of the burden, and their soul is gone into captivity. (Isa 46:1–2)

Second Isaiah devotes a whole chapter to mockery of fallen Babylon, contrasting the glamor and seeming permanence of its former state with the indignity and helplessness that will be its lot when the city falls to its attackers:

> Come down and sit in the dust: O virgin, daughter Babel, sit on the ground: there is no throne, O daughter of the Chaldeans; for thou shalt no more be called, Tender and delicate. Take the millstones, and grind meal; loose thy locks: make bare the feet: uncover the leg, and pass through the floods. Thy filthiness shall be discovered, and thy shame shall be seen: I will take vengeance, and I will not meet thee as a man. Our redeemer, the Lord of hosts is his Name, the holy One of Israel. Sit still, and get thee into darkness, O daughter of the Chaldeans; for thou shalt no more be called, The lady of kingdoms. I was wroth with my people: I have polluted mine inheritance, and given them into thine hand, thou didst show them no mercy, but thou didst lay thy very heavy yoke upon the ancient. And thou saidest, I shall be a lady forever, so that thou didst not set thy mind to these things, neither didst thou remember the latter end thereof. Therefore now hear, thou that art given to pleasures, and dwellest careless, She saith in her heart, I am and none else: I shall not sit as a widow, neither shall I know the loss of children. But these two things shall come to thee suddenly on one day, the loss of children and widowhood; they shall come upon thee in their perfection, for the multitude of thy divinations, and for the great abundance of thine enchanters. For thou hast trusted in thy wickedness; thou hast said, None seeth me. Thy wisdom and thy knowledge, they have caused thee to rebel, and thou hast said in thine heart, I am, and none else. Therefore shall evil come upon thee, and thou shalt not know the morning thereof; destruction shall fall upon thee, which thou shalt not be able to put away: destruction shall come upon thee suddenly, or

> thou beware. Stand now among thine enchanters, and in the multitude of thy soothsayers (with whom thou hast wearied thyself from thy youth) if so be thou mayest have profit, or if so be thou mayest have strength. Thou art wearied in the multitude of thy counsels: let now the astrologers, the stargazers, and prognosticators stand up, and save thee from these things that shall come upon thee. Behold, they shall be as stubble: the fire shall burn them; they shall not deliver their own lives from the power of the flame: there shall be no coals to warm at, nor light to sit by. Thus shall they serve thee, with whom thou hast wearied thee, even thy merchants from thy youth; every one shall wander to his own quarters: none shall save thee. (Isa 47:1–12)[4]

This robust tirade against Babylon has a timeless quality. It could be addressed to any of the great powers that have exercised hegemony over the world for a time. Their fantasy of exceptionalism led them to believe that they were not subject to the usual vicissitudes of history. Their delusion did not save them. They inevitably fell into decline. It is as though the prophet was saying to the dominant power of his time, "You may be rich and powerful now, but the time will come, and even now is coming, when the situation will be reversed and you will fall into obloquy." The dominance of Babylon was an affront to God, and the prophet puts into its mouth words that belong only to God: "I am and no other." Its self-sufficiency is blasphemous. All the acquisitions and accomplishments that seemed to set it above others will be lost, and the city will be left despoiled, impoverished, and despised—forlorn.

In a demonstration of a certain geopolitical acuity, Second Isaiah points to the Persian leader Kurush or Cyrus II (c. 590–

---

[4] Another celebration of Babylon's fall can be found in Jeremiah 50—51. See also Revelation 18.

530 BCE) as the instrument by which God's plan of salvation will be realized. Cyrus was a successful military leader, but also a respectful and benevolent governor of the peoples he conquered.[5] In October 539 BCE, he entered Babylon and gained thereby hegemony not only over Mesopotamia but also over Syria and Palestine, both of which had fallen into the hands of the Babylonians. As Second Isaiah predicted, his victory led to the liberation of the Jewish captives. This was noted in Ezra:

> Now in the first year of Cyrus, King of Persia, that the word of the Lord spoken by the mouth of Jeremiah might be accomplished, the Lord stirred up the spirit of Cyrus, King of Persia, and he made a proclamation through all his kingdom, and also by writing, saying, Thus saith Cyrus King of Persia, The Lord God of Heaven hath given me all the kingdoms of the earth, and he hath commanded me to build him an house in Jerusalem, which is in Judah. Who is he among you of all his people with whom his God is, let him go up to Jerusalem which is in Judah, and build the house of the Lord God of Israel, he is the God, which is in Jerusalem. And everyone that remaineth in any place where he sojourneth, let them of his place relieve him with silver and gold, and with substance, and with cattle and with a willing offering, for the house of God that is in Jerusalem. (Ezra 1:1–4)

To a community disheartened by their loss of homeland and threatened by a loss of national identity and of the privileges that went with it, the prophet points to a new phenomenon: Cyrus's spectacular victories in the 540s and the consequent expansion of Persian rule. Cyrus is not only a high achiever, he is also God's chosen instrument. "I call a bird from the East, and the man of my

---

[5] A contemporaneous narrative of his peaceful entry into Babylon and his benevolent rule is found on the Cyrus Cylinder, now in the British Museum.

counsel from far: as I have spoken, so will I bring it to pass: I have purposed it, and I will do it" (Isa 46:11). And thus, "He saith to Cyrus, Thou art my shepherd, and he shall perform all my desire: saying also to Jerusalem, Thou shalt be built, and to the Temple, Thy foundation shall be surely laid" (44:28). "I have raised him up in righteousness, and I will direct all his ways: he shall build my city, and he shall let go my captives, not for price nor reward, saith the Lord of hosts" (45:13).

> I have raised up from the North, and he shall come: from the East sun shall he call upon my name, and shall come upon princes as upon clay, and as the potter treadeth mire under the foot. (Isa 41:25)

> Thus saith the Lord unto Cyrus his anointed, whose right hand I have holden to subdue nations before him: therefore will I weaken the loins of kings, and open the doors before him, and the gates shall not be shut. I will go before thee, and make the crooked straight: I will break the brazen doors, and burst the iron bars. And I will give thee the treasures of darkness, and the things hid in secret places, that thou mayest know that I am the Lord which call thee by thy name, even the God of Israel. For Jacob my servant's sake, and Israel mine elect, I will even call thee by thy name, and name thee, though thou hast not known me. I am the Lord, and there is none other; there is no God besides me: I girded thee, though thou hast not known me. That they may know from the rising of the sun, and from the West, that there is none besides me. I am the Lord, and there is none other. (Isa 45:1–6)

This deliverance by the hand of a foreigner has a revelatory function. It will manifest to faithless Israelites that God remains faithful even when they do not. The seemingly impossible prospect of liberation poses no problem for God. "The captive hasteneth to be loosed, and that he should not die in the pit, nor that his bread should fail" (51:14).

> Shall the prey be taken from the mighty? or the just captivity delivered? But thus saith the Lord, Even the captivity of the mighty shall be taken away: and the prey of the tyrant shall be delivered: for I will contend with him that contendeth with thee, and I will save thy children, And I will feed them that spoil thee, with their own flesh, and they shall be drunken with their own blood, as with sweet wine; and all flesh shall know that I the Lord am thy Saviour and thy Redeemer, the mighty one of Jacob. (Isa 49:25–26)

Departure from Babylon is only the first step in the process of returning to the land promised to their ancestors. Even though the valleys are raised and the mountains made low, the journey of more than six hundred miles through unfriendly country will be hazardous. The Lord promises to protect them on their journey.

> When thou passest through the waters, I will be with thee, and through the floods, that they do not overflow thee. When thou walkest through the very fire, thou shalt not be burnt, neither shall the flame kindle upon thee. (Isa 43:2)

> Fear not, for I am with thee: I will bring thy seed from the East, and gather thee from the West. I will say to the North, Give: and to the South, Keep not back: bring my sons from far, and my daughters from the ends of the earth. Everyone shall be called by my Name: for I created him for my glory, formed him and made him. I will bring forth the blind people, and they shall have eyes, and the deaf, and they shall have ears. (Isa 43:5–8)

This protection involves dramatic changes to the environment through which the people must pass. It is as though material creation will be called upon to facilitate the progress of God's people to their promised destiny. Potential impediments to their progress will be eliminated; participation in the journey will not be limited to the bold and the brave; there will be a place also for the blind and the weak.

> I will make waste mountains, and hills, and dry up all their herbs, and I will make the floods islands, and I will dry up the pools. And I will bring the blind by a way, that they knew not, and lead them by paths that they have not known: I will make darkness light before them, and crooked things straight. These things will I do unto them, and not forsake them. (Isa 42:15–16)

> When the poor and the needy seek water, and there *is* none (their tongue faileth for thirst: I the Lord will hear them: I the God of Israel will not forsake them:) I will open rivers in the tops of the hills, and fountains in the midst of the valleys: I will make the wilderness as a pool of water, and the waste land as springs of water. I will set in the wilderness the cedar, the Shittah, and the myrrh tree, and the pine tree, and I will set in the wilderness the fir tree, the elm and the box tree together. Therefore let them see and know, and let them consider and understand together that the hand of the Lord hath done this, and the holy One of Israel hath created it. (Isa 41:17–20)

A moratorium is declared for the natural order so as to provide safe passage for the chosen people; the wildest of animals will hold back in deference to the command of their Maker.

> Behold, I do a new thing: now shall it come forth: shall you not know it? I will even make a way in the desert,

> and floods in the wilderness. The wild beasts shall honor me, the dragons and the ostriches, because I gave water in the desert, and floods in the wilderness to give drink to my people, even to mine elect. (Isa 43:19–20)

The manner of God's dealing with the people can be seen as a portent of the way in which all peoples will find salvation when the acceptable time arrives. The hand of the Lord is not shortened (cf. 50:2); the divine liberating impulse is not exhausted by this one act of emancipation. What God did then can be done again when another day of salvation dawns:

> Thus saith the Lord, In an acceptable time have I heard thee, and in a day of salvation have I helped thee: and I will preserve thee, and will give thee for a covenant of the people, that thou mayest raise up the earth, and obtain the inheritance of the desolate heritages: That thou mayest say to the prisoners, Go forth; and to them that are in darkness, Show yourselves; they shall feed in the ways, and their pastures shall be in all the tops of the hills. They shall not be hungry, neither shall they be thirsty, neither shall the heat smite them, nor the sun, for he that hath compassion on them, shall lead them; even to the springs of water shall he drive them. And I will make all my mountains, as a way, and my paths shall be exalted. (Isa 49:8–11)

Not only will the exiles return from captivity, but the scattered children of Israel will return from other regions to which they have been dispersed (49:12, 49:22–23). Israel will enjoy a prolific increase, an infallible guarantee of divine blessing:

> For thy desolations, and thy waste places, and thy land destroyed, shall surely be now narrow for them that shall dwell in it, and they that dwell devour thee, shall be far

> away. The children of thy barrenness shall say again in thine ears, the place is strait for me: give place to me that I may dwell. Then shalt thou say in thine heart, Who hath begotten me these, seeing I am barren and desolate, a captive and a wanderer to and fro? and who hath nourished them? behold, I was left alone: whence are these? (Isa 49:19–21)

The present state of desolation will be followed not by mere survival or a return to what was before the destruction of Jerusalem. It will be a time of extravagant material prosperity, peace, and righteousness in which, as Jeremiah predicted, all would be instructed by the Lord, with the *torah* written in their hearts (cf. Jer 31:33–34).

> O thou afflicted and tossed with tempest, that hast no comfort, behold, I will lay thy stones with the carbuncle, and lay thy foundation with sapphires, And I will make thy windows of emeralds, and thy gates shining stones, and all thy borders of pleasant stones. And all thy children shall be taught of the Lord, and much peace shall be to thy children. In righteousness shalt thou be established, and be far from oppression; for thou shalt not fear it: and from fear; for it shall not come near thee. (Isa 54:11–14)

Superabundance, the hallmark of divine salvation, is evident here. Not only in tangible endowments, but also in the ample consolation afforded by the Lord, as promised in the opening verses of Second Isaiah. The result is joy and gladness and the spontaneous outbursting of songs of praise:

> Surely the Lord shall comfort Zion: he shall comfort all her desolations, and he shall make her desert like Eden, and her wilderness like the garden of the Lord: joy and

> gladness shall be found therein: praise, and the voice of singing. (Isa 51:3)

Nor will this be a transitory state, subject to future threats. God will cement the benevolent relationship with an everlasting covenant, similar to that made to Noah, a comprehensive covenant from which none will be excluded. It will be the mission of Israel, as God's servant, to be a light to all nations, to bring the Gentiles into the ambit of God's gracious fidelity so that all creation will redound to the glory of the Lord:

> For this is unto me as the waters of Noah; for as I have sworn that the waters of Noah should no more go over the earth, so have I sworn that I would not be angry with thee, nor rebuke thee. For the mountains shall remove, and the hills shall fall down; but my mercy shall not depart from thee, neither shall the covenant of my peace fall away, saith the Lord, that hath compassion on thee. (Isa 54:9–10)

The deliverance that God will bring about and that the prophet proclaims far exceeds the initial act by which it is demonstrated. At least some of the exiles did return to Palestine in the immediate aftermath of Babylon's overthrow. But the prophet seems to be envisaging an ampler gospel—good news that went beyond the immediate circumstances for which it was intended. No doubt, the initiative begun by Cyrus radically failed to live up to the seemingly glorious prospect described in the prophetic oracles, but it was a step in the right direction and, crucially, did secure the continuance of Israel as a nation and, thereby, the possibility of fulfilling its mission.

As it was proclaimed in the sixth century before Christ, the book of Second Isaiah was inserted into the whole history of God's dealings with the chosen people. The primary level of interpretation and understanding must take this very seriously:

> The theological fundament of the coming salvation is historical. The election of Israel by Yahwe created a particular relation between God and his nation. Although the election is an historical deed from the past, it is still effective. As focuses of the history of election the prophet considers above all the deliverance out of Egypt and the vocation of Abraham. By the election Yahwe became the God of Israel. Israel became a nation through him, so that he is its maker, creator and former. Yahwe rightly regards Israel as his own people, which is sanctified by his belonging to the holy Yahwe. The relationship which originates in this way makes Israel an *'ebed yhwh*, who rightly expects that Yahwe will help and save him in his distress. For Yahwe is Israel's *go'el*: he has undertaken the obligation to redeem Israel when strangers have it in their power. In other words, between Yahwe and Israel there is a bond of *chesed*.[6]

For us who read the book in a different era and from a different perspective, it inevitably intimates a broader message that for Christian readers echoes the New Testament. The lesson we can learn from the prophet is that the salvation promised us by God is not a thin "spiritual" benefit that is mainly concerned with releasing us from the effects due to the wrong choices we have made and the sins that mar our integrity. The prophet invites us to a more holistic notion of what salvation means. It is not a matter of individual acquittal from just punishment, but the renewal and transformation of the whole of creation: a new heaven and a new earth. And a corresponding implementation of God's plan for humanity sketched out for us in the Book of Genesis, before the fall. All things will be made new, beyond our deserving and even beyond our imagining. This is the bold message that Second Isaiah proclaimed to a people on the cusp of extinction. And we,

---

[6] Simplified from Schoors, *I Am God Your Saviour*, 172.

people of faith in another generation, are beneficiaries of the same promise.

> Surely as the rain cometh down, and the snow from heaven, and returneth not thither but watereth the earth, and maketh it to bring forth and bud, that it may give seed to the sower, and bread unto him that eateth, So shall my word be, that goeth out of my mouth: it shall not return unto me void, but it shall accomplish that which I will, and it shall prosper in the thing whereto I sent it. Therefore ye shall go out with joy, and be led forth with peace; the mountains and the hills shall break forth before you into joy, and all the trees of the field shall clap their hands. For thorns there shall grow fir trees; for nettles shall grow the myrrh tree, and it shall be to the Lord for a name, and for an everlasting sign that shall not be taken away. (Isa 55:8–13)

To us also is addressed the admonition, "Fear not, for I am with thee" (43:1–5).